Make Your Own Last Will & Testament

A Special Request

Your brief Amazon review could really helps us!
The link below will take you to the Amazon.com review page for this book. Please leave a review.

www.estate-bee.com/review9

Estate Bee

By EstateBee Publishing

Bibliographic Data

- International Standard Book Number (ISBN): 978-1-913889-12-8
- Printed in the United States of America
- First Edition: December 2010
- Second Edition: January 2014
- Third Edition: December 2020 (Updated January 2025)

Published By: EstateBee Limited
33 Canonbie Road
London SE23 3AW
United Kingdom

Printed and Distributed By: Kindle Direct Publishing, an Amazon Company

For more information, e-mail books@estate-bee.com.

Important Note

This book is meant as a general guide to preparing your own last will and testament. While effort has been made to make this book as accurate as possible, laws and their interpretation are constantly changing. As such, you are advised to update this information with your own research and/or counsel and to consult with your personal legal, financial, and/or medical advisors before acting on any information contained in this book.

The purpose of this book is to educate and entertain. It is not meant to provide legal, financial, or medical advice or to create any attorney-client or other advisory relationship. The authors and publisher shall have neither liability (whether in negligence or otherwise) nor responsibility to any person or entity with respect to any loss or damage caused or alleged to be caused directly or indirectly by the information contained in this book or the use of that information.

About EstateBee

EstateBee, the international self-help legal publisher, was founded in 2000 by lawyers from one of the most prestigious international law firms in the World.

Our aim was simple - to provide access to quality legal information and products at an affordable price.

Our will writing software was first published in that year and, following its adaptation to cater for the legal systems of various countries worldwide, quickly drew more than 40,000 visitors per month to our website. From this humble start, EstateBee has quickly grown to become a leading international estate planning and asset protection self-help publisher with legal titles in the United States, Canada, the United Kingdom, Australia, and Ireland.

Our publications provide customers with the confidence and knowledge to help them deal with everyday estate planning issues such as the preparation of a last will and testament, a living trust, a power of attorney, administering an estate and much more.

By providing customers with much needed information and forms, we enable them to place themselves in a position where they can protect both themselves and their families using easy to read legal documents and forward planning techniques.

The Future....

We are always seeking to expand and improve the products and services we offer. However, to do this, we need to hear from interested authors and to receive feedback from our customers.

If something isn't clear to you in one of our publications, please let us know and we'll try to make it clearer in the next edition. If you can't find the answer you want and have a suggestion for an addition to our range, we'll happily look at that too.

Using Self-Help Books

Before using a self-help book, you need to carefully consider the advantages and disadvantages of doing so – particularly where the subject matter is of a legal or tax related nature.

In writing our self-help books, we try to provide readers with an overview of the laws in a specific area, as well as some sample documents. While this overview is often general in nature, it provides a good starting point for those wishing to carry out a more detailed review of a topic.

However, unlike an attorney advising a client, we cannot cover every conceivable eventuality that might affect our readers. Within the intended scope of this book, we can only cover the principal areas in each topic, and even where we cover these areas, we can still only do so to a moderate extent. To do otherwise would result in the writing of a textbook which would be capable of use by legal professionals. This is not what we do.

We try to present useful information and documents that can be used by an average reader with little or no legal knowledge. While our sample documents can be used in most cases, everybody's personal circumstances are different. As such, they may not be suitable for everyone. You may have personal circumstances which might impact the effectiveness of these documents or even your desire to use them. The reality is that without engaging an attorney to review your personal circumstances, this risk will always exist. It's for this very reason that you need to consider whether the cost of using a do-it-yourself legal document outweighs the risk that there may be something special about your particular circumstances which might not be taken into account by the sample documents attached to this book (or indeed any other sample documents).

It goes without saying (we hope) that if you are in any doubt as to whether the documents in this book are suitable for use in your particular circumstances, you should contact a suitably qualified attorney for advice before using them. Remember the decision to use these documents is yours. We are not advising you in any respect.

In using this book, you should also consider the fact that this book has been written with the purpose of providing a general overview of the laws in the United States. As such, it does not attempt to cover all the various procedural nuances and specific requirements that may apply from state to state – although we do point some of these out along the way. Rather, in our book, we try to provide forms which give a fair example of the type of forms which are commonly used in most states. Nevertheless, it remains possible that your state may have specific requirements which have not been taken into account in our forms.

Another thing that you should remember is that the law changes – thousands of new laws are brought into force every day and, by the same token, thousands are repealed or amended every day. As such, it is possible that while you are reading this book, the law might well have been changed. We hope it hasn't, but the chance does exist. To address this, when we become aware of them, we do send updates to our customers about material changes to the law. We also ensure that our books are reviewed and revised regularly to take account of these changes.

Anyway, assuming that all the above is acceptable to you, let's move on to exploring the topic at hand..........last wills and testaments.

Table of Contents

CHAPTER 5
Appointing Executors

CHAPTER 6
Guardians and Children

CHAPTER 7
Estate Planning

Preface
An Introduction to Wills

A will, more formally known as a last will and testament, is a legal document that allows you to express your wishes and intentions regarding the distribution of your estate following your death. Your estate consists of all property that you own at the time of your death (such as real estate, land, cash, stocks, bonds, jewelry, furniture, clothing, and artwork) less any debts that you owe. It is your will that sets out how this property will be divided between your relatives, friends, and charities after you die.

As well as setting out how you want your estate to be divided, you can also use your will for several other related functions. For example, under your will you can nominate someone (known as an executor or personal representative) to take responsibility for winding up your estate after you die and distributing your assets in accordance with the terms of your will. You can also appoint someone to take care of your children as well as establish trusts for their benefit and welfare. You can even set out your wishes regarding anatomical gifts and the type of funeral arrangements you would like.

As your will has legal status, both your executors and your heirs will be required to abide by its terms when dealing with your estate. Even where a challenge is made to your will or a dispute arises in connection with its interpretation, courts will generally do their upmost to give effect to the terms of your will as you originally intended.

For those with sizeable estates, a will can also play a strategic role in tax planning. The manner in which your property is passed to your beneficiaries, how much of it is passed, and when and to whom it is passed can all have an impact on the taxation of both your estate and the beneficiaries who receive it. A carefully drafted will can minimize death taxes, estate taxes, transfer costs and even the general costs of probate.

If you do not make a valid will, not only will you lose out on the opportunity for tax planning, your estate will be divided in a set manner prescribed under state intestacy laws. These laws set out who is entitled to receive from your estate and in what proportions. Where state intestacy laws apply, there is a very real risk that your estate will not be distributed according to your wishes.

In some cases, failing to update your will can be as problematic as not making one at all. Events will most likely occur in your lifetime which create a need to change the provisions of your will. These events may arise because of changes in the law, in your financial circumstances, in the value of your assets or even in your desire to gift assets to certain beneficiaries. If your will is not updated to address these changes, they can have significant unintended consequences - particularly with respect to the way your assets are ultimately divided amongst your family members.

Some typical changes in circumstances that can cause unintended consequences if not addressed include:

- birth of new family members.
- death of intended beneficiaries.
- significant changes in beneficiaries' circumstances.
- changes in your relationships (such as marriage or divorce).
- acquisition of new assets.
- substantial appreciation in value of existing assets.
- disposal or substantial depreciation in value or loss of certain existing assets.

To ensure similar changes in circumstances are addressed in your will, it is recommended that you review and update your will annually or, at the very least, every two to three years. It is also recommended that you review your will whenever there is a significant change in your personal circumstances.

Did You Know

The English Statute of Wills in 1540 first allowed landowners to dispose of their land after their death using a written document known as a 'Will'. Personal property (all property other than land) was bequeathed in a document known as 'Testament'. The terms subsequently merged into 'last will and testament'. This was ultimately shortened in modern usage to the word 'will'.

CHAPTER 1

About Wills

Definition of a Will

A will is a legal declaration by which a person gives instructions to his executors, heirs, and beneficiaries about the disposition of his property after his death. It is generally comprised of several specific components or features and can come in several forms. We look at each in the ensuing pages.

Did You Know

As the author of a will, you will generally be referred to as the testator as you are 'attesting' to your wishes. Sometimes, you will see the female designation of testator (i.e. testatrix), but often, the term is gender neutral. After you have died, you will be known as the deceased or the decedent. If you die without a valid will, you will be said to have died intestate.

Basic Clauses of a Will

Most wills are comprised of several essential clauses – those clauses that you would expect to see in virtually every will. These essential clauses are usually supplemented and personalized by several ancillary clauses that are specific to the testator's personal circumstances.

Standard wills typically contain the following clauses:

- *Preamble** - sets out the name and addresses of the testator.

- *Revocation** – revokes all previous wills and other testamentary documents made by the testator.

- *Executor** - appoints one or more persons (known as executors or personal representatives) to 'wind up' the testator's estate following his death.

- *Survivorship* –requires beneficiaries under a will to survive the testator by a fixed period, such as 30 days, before becoming entitled to inherit under the testator's will. This clause is commonly used in connection with gifts made between spouses and serves as a means of reducing multiple estate administrations and the possible double payment of estate taxes where both spouses die within a short time of each other.

- *Cash Gift (legacy)* – makes a gift of cash.

- *Specific Property Gift (bequest)* – makes a gift of a specific item of property.

- *Residue Gift** - makes a gift of the balance of the testator's estate after all the cash gifts and specific gifts are made and after all debts and taxes are paid.

- *Estate Administration and Expenses* – specifies how the testator's estate is to pay its debts, expenses, taxes and costs of estate administration.

- *UTMA and Child Trusts* - creates a type of custodianship or trust to manage property gifted by the testator to a young beneficiary under his will.

- *Guardianship* – nominates guardians and successor guardians to care for the testator's minor children and to manage property that they might receive.

- *Executive Powers** - sets out the powers to be granted to the executors, which will be in addition to any powers that they might be granted under federal or state law.

- *Executors' Fees & Liabilities* – specifies whether the executors should be compensated for their work as executors and whether they should be held liable if they negligently cause a depletion in the value of the estate.

- *Attestation** – the place where the testator signs and executes his will.

- *Witnessing** - the place where the witnesses (usually two) sign and attest that they have witnessed the testator sign his will in their presence.

The clauses with the asterisk (*) above are clauses that should appear in every will.

We will discuss more about each of these above clauses over the course of this book. However, for the moment, it is sufficient that you are simply made aware of them for background informational purposes.

Types of Wills

There are numerous different types of wills in use today. Some are legally recognized in all states, while others are only recognized in a few specific states. If you plan on making a specific type of will and are in any doubt as to whether that type of will is valid in your state, be sure to check with your attorney or local state statute before making the will. Otherwise, you run the risk of it being invalid or unenforceable in your state – in which case the rules of intestacy could apply.

The main types of wills currently in use include:

Standard Wills

This is arguably the most common type of will made in the United States and, as its name implies, is relatively straightforward. It usually only provides for (i) the distribution of the testator's estate, (ii) the appointment of an executor, and, if required, (iii) the appointment of guardians to care for the testator's minor children.

Testamentary Trust Wills

This is a will that provides for the creation of a trust upon the testator's death, usually for the benefit of the testator's spouse or young children. Once the trust has been created, the terms of the testator's will usually provide for the automatic and immediate transfer of some or all his assets into that trust. Once the assets are transferred to the trust, they will be managed on behalf of the trust's beneficiaries by the persons named in the testator's will as trustees. The specific way the trust assets are to be managed and the powers of the trustees to do so are usually set out in the will.

Pour-Over Wills

This is a will that has the primary purpose of providing for the transfer of some or all the testator's assets to a pre-existing trust upon his death. In most cases, this trust will be a 'living trust' which has been independently set up under a trust deed, which has trustees appointed under that deed to manage the trust assets and which has specific provisions relating to the actual management and distribution of assets received by that trust.

Self-Proving Wills

In the normal course of probating an estate, (i.e. winding it up), either a family member of the testator or the person named as executor in the testator's will presents the will to the probate court. The probate court will then seek to determine its authenticity to ensure it is in fact the testator's will. If there is any doubt as to the authenticity of the testator's signature on the will, the court may call upon the persons who witnessed the testator sign the will to certify that his signature is authentic and that the will was validly executed.

To avoid having to call witnesses to court in this manner, the testator and the witnesses often 'pre-validate' the testator's signature by signing a document called a 'self-proving affidavit'. This affidavit is little more than a declaration signed by the witnesses acknowledging that they witnessed the testator sign his will (the same acknowledgement that they would give when witnessing the testator's will in any event). However, the big difference between the two documents is that the self-proving affidavit is signed in the presence of a notary who, in turn, officially seals the document to give it authenticity. Once the affidavit is sealed, it is attached to the related will which, in turn, becomes known as a 'self-proving will'. The court will normally accept a testator's signature as being authentic where it is contained within a self-proving will of this type.

Holographic Wills

This is a will that has been written in the testator's own handwriting but, unlike most other wills, does not need to be witnessed. This type of will is not valid in every state and we generally recommend that you avoid using these types of wills if possible.

Oral Wills

As the name suggests, this is a will that is verbally spoken rather than written down on paper. Very few states recognize the validity of such wills and those that do only permit an oral will where it is made during a final illness and with respect to personal property (i.e. property such as cash, stocks, personal belongings, etc., but excluding land and buildings) which has a relatively low monetary value.

Joint Wills

A joint will is a single document incorporating the instructions of two people, usually spouses or domestic partners, who wish to gift their respective estates to each other if they die. The will stipulates how the estate of the first person to die will be distributed following his or her death, as well as how the estate of the survivor will be distributed when he or she dies. When the first person dies, the will becomes irrevocable and incapable of being changed. This, therefore, places enormous restrictions on the ability of the surviving person to change his mind about how or to whom the assets in his or her estate will pass upon his or her death. As a result, we do not recommend the use of joint wills and suggest the use of two separate wills in their place. If you plan on using a joint will, we suggest you consult an attorney.

Mirror Wills

Mirror wills are wills which mirror the terms of each other. They are usually made by spouses or civil partners who wish to leave everything they own to the other if they die or if both die together, to specific named beneficiaries. Unlike joint wills, mirror wills are made on two separate documents and, as such, the parties are free to change the terms of their will at any time and in any manner they deem fit. For this reason, the use of mirror wills is generally recommended over joint wills.

Living Wills

Despite its name, this is not a last will and testament. While a normal will deals with the distribution of a deceased person's property following his death, a living will is used to let doctors and other healthcare providers know the types of life sustaining medical treatment that the author wants and doesn't want to receive if he is terminally ill or in a state of permanent unconsciousness and unable to communicate his own wishes. Living wills, in varying degrees, are valid in all states.

Dying Without a Will

If you die without making a will, you will be said to have died intestate. The same applies if you make a will but following your death it cannot be located, is deemed false, or is deemed invalid for not meeting the relevant statutory requirements for valid wills. Every state has statutory rules setting out how a person's property will be distributed if they are deemed to have died intestate. The application of these rules could result in the distribution of your property in a manner contrary to what you would have wanted had you been able to make the choice - so dying intestate is a situation best avoided.

For example, under the intestacy laws of most states, the general rule of thumb is that the first in line to benefit from your death will be your surviving spouse and children. If, however, you die without leaving a surviving spouse or children, then the general rule of thumb is 'the bigger your estate is, the more distant the relatives who get to share in it'.

The law sets out certain formalities that must be followed for a will to be valid. These formalities relate to the wording, witnessing, and signing of a will, as well as to the mental capacity of the person making it. If you make a will that does not comply with the applicable legal requirements for making a will in your state, the probate court could ultimately declare it to be invalid. In such cases, you will be treated as if you had died intestate. To ensure that this does not happen, and that the provisions expressed in your will are carried out, these legal requirements and formalities must be strictly observed.

The validity of a will is usually determined by the probate court. When a will is admitted to the probate court as part of the probate procedure (the legal process of determining the validity of a will and setting an estate), the court will make a determination as to whether the will is genuine and has been validly executed before it will make any rulings in relation to the distribution of the testator's estate. If it is ruled invalid, the rules of intestacy will apply.

In several states, such as Arizona, Texas, and Wisconsin, the process of validating wills can be simplified through the use of self-proved wills. Executors can submit wills that include signed affidavits from the testator and witnesses, affirming that the will was properly executed, to the probate court. These affidavits are typically accepted as evidence of the will's validity, streamlining the probate process. Other states, such as South Carolina, Vermont, and Wyoming, require wills to undergo full probate proceedings, where the court formally rules on the will's validity. Executors are advised to check local laws, as wills generally need to be filed within a specific period following the testator's death. Failure to meet this deadline may result in the will being deemed invalid, in which case the deceased's estate will be distributed according to the rules of intestacy rather than the provisions of the will.

As well as providing how a deceased person's property is to be divided following his death, the laws of intestacy also set out who will be entitled to act as the administrator of the deceased's estate. The administrator is the person who will be legally responsible for distributing the deceased's estate in accordance with the rules of intestacy. His role is, in many ways, like that of an executor. The probate court will normally appoint the person who stands to gain the most from the deceased's estate under state intestacy laws as the administrator.

Intestacy is discussed in greater detail in Chapter 3.

Do-It-Yourself Wills

While you can easily obtain will forms and other legal document forms in a 'fill-in-the-blanks' format online or from various stores, we recommend that you take extreme care in determining which forms to use and which to ignore. Your personal and financial circumstances will grow in complexity as you age and, as such, your changing needs might not be sufficiently addressed by a 'one-size fits all' form. This is true particularly where you have a large estate such as one which exceeds the value of the current estate tax thresholds (see Chapter 8) or where you have complex business and financial interests.

However, if your estate is 'normal' then, in many cases, these documents can suffice. For example, if a husband and wife wished to leave everything to each other in the event of the other's death, or in the event that both died at the same time, to their children, a 'do-it-yourself will' can suffice. This is because the distributions are relatively straightforward. Similarly, if you simply wish to make normal gifts (real estate, cash, art, etc.) to your family and friends, these types of wills are also generally accepted in 'do-it-yourself' format.

It is possible that the use of sub-standard 'do-it-yourself wills' can lead to confusion in the interpretation of your will, delays in distributions and unwanted tax consequences. In one well-known case, a do-it-yourself testator wrote "I leave all my personal property to my wife". Endless chaos ensued because the law distinguishes 'real property' (land and real estate) from 'personal property' (all property other than land and real estate, but including leasehold property, such as cash, antiques, etc.). Here, the bulk of the estate was in the form of freehold land, which was not literally dealt with under the will, and could have been split between various relatives upon intestacy. In this particular case, the widow had to go through the trauma, delay, and considerable expense of seeking a declaration that her husband intended her to inherit his real estate, as well as his personal estate which was not of great value in this instance.

Important Note

While all of EstateBee's legal documents are drafted to a very high standard and approved by lawyers, in the absence of being able to examine your personal circumstances in detail, we have no way of knowing whether they are completely suitable for your particular circumstances. As such, you still need to use our documents with care and the decision to use them is yours. If you are in any doubt as to their suitability for you, speak with an attorney.

If you are happy to draft a do-it-yourself will, we recommend that you carefully consider the use of such a document in the context of your overall situation and personal circumstances. If you have any doubt or concern as to the suitability of a particular document for your circumstances, you should consult a suitably qualified attorney before you sign it. Consulting an attorney is the best way to ensure you do not end up with messy, unintended consequences. The price you will pay for peace of mind — and the assurance that those you want to inherit will inherit — will be more than worth it.

Making a Will Without a Lawyer

In all states, a lawyer's involvement is not required for you to draft your will. If your situation is not a complicated one, and you simply want to make gifts, appoint guardians and executors under your will, then preparing your own will should not be very difficult, provided that you have some good self-help materials on hand. But as with most do-it-yourself kits, if your situation is complex or is unusual in some way, you should consult an attorney.

CHAPTER 2

Making a Valid Will

Elements of a Valid Will

While most state laws do not expressly require a specific format for a will, virtually all states have minimum elements that must be present for a will to be deemed valid. In general, for a will to be deemed valid, it must:

- be made by a person who has reached the age of majority in his state. There are some exceptions to this general rule which we will discuss below.

- be made by a person voluntarily and without pressure from any other person. For this reason, it is not advisable for a potential beneficiary to be present when you instruct your lawyer to draft your will. Additionally, it is not advisable to provide any gifts to your attorney in your will if he or she has drafted your will.

- be made by a person who is of 'sound and disposing mind'.

- be in writing (normally).

- be signed by the testator in the presence of two witnesses..

- be signed by all the witnesses in the presence of the testator (after he or she has signed it) and in the presence of each other. A beneficiary under the will or the spouse of such a beneficiary should not act as a witness to the signing of the will. If such a beneficiary or the spouse of such a beneficiary act as a witness, the gift to the beneficiary under the will could be deemed to be invalid, although the will itself should remain valid.

- include an attestation clause.

- be notarized if made in the state of Louisiana.

Age of Majority

The age of majority is a legal description that denotes the threshold age at which a person ceases to be a minor and subsequently becomes legally responsible for his own actions and decisions. It is the age at which the responsibility of the minor's parents or guardians over him is relinquished. Reaching the age of majority also has several important practical consequences for the minor. The minor is now legally entitled to do certain things which he could not legally do before reaching the age of majority. For example, he is now legally entitled to enter binding contracts, hold significant assets, buy stocks and shares, vote in elections, buy consume alcohol, etc. Upon reaching the age of 18, the former minor will also be entitled to make a will.

It is a general rule in each state that a person must reach the age of 18, or the age of majority in their home state, before being entitled to make a valid legal will. The chart below demonstrates the age of majority as defined by each state.

Age of Majority in the United States	
Age 18	Alaska, Arizona, California, Colorado, Connecticut, District of Columbia, Florida, Georgia, Hawaii, Idaho, Illinois, Indiana, Iowa, Kansas, Kentucky, Louisiana, Maine, Maryland, Massachusetts, Michigan, Minnesota, Missouri, Montana, New Hampshire, New Mexico, New Jersey, New York, North Carolina, North Dakota, Oklahoma, Oregon, Pennsylvania, Rhode Island, South Carolina, South Dakota, Texas, Vermont, Washington, West Virginia and Wyoming.
Age 19	Alabama, Delaware, and Nebraska.
Age 21	Mississippi.
Graduation or 18 – (whichever occurs first)	Ohio and Utah.
Graduation or 18 (whichever occurs later)	Arkansas, Tennessee, and Virginia.

Graduation or 18 – (whichever occurs first) or 19 if still at school	Nevada and Wisconsin.

There are some exceptions to this general rule. For example, some states have a lower age limit such as Louisiana which has a minimum age of 16 years while Georgia has a minimum age of 14 years. Typically, a person under the age of majority who is already married, or who has been married, is also deemed of sufficient age to execute a will. Emancipated minors may also execute a will. An underage person who joins the military or is on active military service can also make a will in many states, as can a seaman or naval officer at sea.

A court can specifically authorize a minor to make a will after a successful application by the minor's parents or guardians. This might be approved, for example, where a minor inherited a large amount of money, invented some innovative computer software, or created the next 'Facebook'. In each case, if the minor is shown to have adequate capacity and the move is deemed prudent, the court will usually consider granting approval for the application.

Mental Capacity

To make a valid legal will, you must typically be of sound and disposing mind and memory. While what constitutes being of 'sound and disposing mind and memory' differs slightly from state to state, it generally means someone who understands:

- what a will is.
- that he is making a will.
- the general extent of his property.
- who his heirs and family members are.
- the way in which his will proposes to distribute his property.

It is important to note that the testator must be of sound mind and memory when he executes a will, not immediately prior to his death. As such, if the testator ends up suffering from any kind of mental impairment such as dementia or Alzheimer's disease, or even from an addiction to drugs or alcohol, the court will look at the testator's mental state at the time he executed his will in order to determine whether it is valid. If it can be shown that testator was not mentally impaired or under the influence at that time, the court will most likely deem the will valid in so far as mental capacity is concerned. If the testator is suffering from any such impairments prior to executing a will, it is advisable that he visit his doctor on the day he executes his will (or even that he executes it in the doctor's presence) and has the doctor prepare a medical certificate stating that in his or her professional opinion the testator was mentally competent and lucid on that date. These types of statements have a strong persuasive effect on the courts, and generally result in a determination of valid mental capacity.

Undue Influence

Another form of mental incapacity is legally referred to as 'undue influence'. Undue influence is the use of influence by a third party in a position of trust or authority of any kind of control or influence over another person such that the other person signs a contract or other legal instrument (such as a mortgage or deed) which, absent the influence of the third party, he or she would not ordinarily have signed. In other words, any act by a third party that might coerce the free will of the person executing a will creates a presumption of undue influence. A contract or legal instrument may be set aside as non-binding on any party who signs it under undue influence.

Claims of undue influence are often raised by sibling beneficiaries in circumstances where one sibling is bequeathed more from a parent's will than the other siblings. In these situations, an aggrieved beneficiary may use the opportunity to attack and try to overturn the terms of the parent's will. If you plan on leaving unequal amounts to your children then, in order to reduce the likelihood of these types of claims arising, it is often useful to explain and document the reasons why you are doing so. Your note can then be attached to your will to be used as evidence if required.

A second scenario in which claims of undue influence arise is when a testator uses a beneficiary's attorney to draft his will. In such circumstances, aggrieved beneficiaries will often assert that the use of the beneficiary's lawyer is evidence of the influence the beneficiary wielded over the testator and the pressure that the beneficiary put on the testator to make specific provisions in his will. This dilemma is illustrated in the example below.

Example

John constantly visits his uncle Bryan, an 88-year-old retired business tycoon, in the nursing home. During his visits, John continuously urges Bryan to leave his vast business interests to him (to the detriment of Bryan's own children who do not visit as often as they should). John, knowing that Bryan is lonely and depressed, threatens to stop visiting him, stating that Bryan is clearly ungrateful for John's kindness and attention. John finally arrives at the nursing home with his own lawyer, who has never met Bryan before. John remains present while Bryan instructs the lawyer to write a new will in which he purports to leave all his business interests to John.

Ideally, an ethical attorney would never agree to make a will in such circumstances, but it does happen. Therefore, it is always wise to get independent legal advice when you make a will.

Format of a Will

As mentioned in the last chapter, while all states recognize the validity of written wills, certain states will not recognize oral or holographic wills. As such, it is important to ensure that your will is in writing, where required, and complies with the laws of your state.

Signing of a Will

We will explore the formal requirements for signing your will later in this book. However, it is important at this juncture to note that wills need to be signed. You can either sign your will or direct someone to do so on your behalf. Signatures may include marks, initials, a rubber stamp, a 'nick-name', or a former name.

Witnessing the Execution of a Will

While each state has its own laws setting out how the signing of a will should be witnessed, these tend to be quite similar from state to state. A valid will requires that your signature be made at the bottom of your will in the presence of two witnesses. In turn, each witness will need to sign his name underneath your signature and include details of his name (in print format), address and (in some cases) occupation.

Notarizing a Will

A will must only be notarized in the state of Louisiana. Even if notarization is not required in your state, it is a recommended procedure because it can accelerate the admission of your will to probate and increase the chances that it deemed to be valid by the probate court.

With notarization, each of the witnesses sign a document called a 'Self-Proving Affidavit'. This is an affidavit sworn by the witnesses which eliminates the need for them to later testify in court that they witnessed the testator signing his will. This affidavit must be sworn before a notary public in the state in which the will is made.

CHAPTER 3

Wills and Intestacy

Why Everyone Needs a Will

Without making a will setting out how you want your estate divided when you die, the probate court will apply common law rules to determine how your estate should be distributed. This distribution will be made amongst your heirs-at-law and, as such, will not include any non-family members. If you do not have any readily identifiable heirs, it is possible that the state may claim your entire estate. By contrast, when you make a will, you can ensure that your assets and property will be given to family members and other beneficiaries of your choosing. Surprisingly, notwithstanding this, over half of all Americans die without having a valid will.

Benefits of a Will

There is no legal requirement that anyone must make a will. Rather, it is a privilege derived from our legal definition of private property. It is also a way of exercising a degree of personal responsibility after our death. Even for a person with simple financial circumstances, there is no good reason not to have a will.

There are several benefits to having a will. A will:

● allows you to determine how you want your debts settled and assets distributed following your death.

- allows you to choose a representative to wind up your affairs.
- allows you to nominate guardians to care for your minor children.
- allows you to make property management arrangements for young beneficiaries.
- assists in preserving or even enhancing the value of your estate through the incorporation of tax and/or estate planning techniques.

If you do not make a will, a court will distribute your estate in accordance with the standard provisions of state law. This type of intestate distribution is not recommended because it may result in a distribution of assets that is inconsistent with the way you would wish to dispose of your estate.

A Will Saves Money

A correctly written will can have several financial benefits. It can reduce death taxes, thereby leaving more of your estate for your beneficiaries. It gives you the opportunity to appoint a competent person to act as your personal representative rather than appointing a professional executor or trustee who will charge a fee based upon the size of your estate. Your will can provide that your personal representative does not have to post an executor's bond. An executor's bond (probate bond) is sometimes required by a probate court to protect the estate's assets during the administration of the estate. This is a cost borne by the deceased's estate. So, by removing the need to post bond, you will save your estate the expense of having to pay a premium for the bond.

Intestacy and Dying Without a Will

If you fail to make a will, you will be declared intestate after you die. If this happens, the intestacy laws of your state of residence will determine who gets what from your estate. In intestacy, your estate will go to administration and the probate court will appoint an administrator. An administrator, as noted before, is a legal term referring to a person appointed by a court to administer an estate. This person will settle debts, pay any necessary taxes and funeral expenses, and distribute the remainder of your estate to your heirs in accordance with state law. Sometimes the court will appoint a relative as administrator, but most often the administrator appointed to an intestate case is a lawyer with no ties to the estate.

The main purpose of intestate succession law is to allow for the distribution of the deceased's estate in a manner that closely resembles how the average person would have written their will if they took the time to do so. Although well intentioned, state intestacy laws are 'guess work' and, as such, cannot always adequately reflect what the testator would have wanted. Most intestacy laws operate in a general manner, and do not deal with specific items. As such, rather than examining specific items of property and determining the appropriate recipient for each item, courts will generally liquidate the assets and then divide the cash among the beneficiaries identified by statute.

Partial Intestacy

As well as providing for the situation where a person fails to make a will, intestacy laws also apply to any portion of your property not dealt with in your will. This is called a partial intestacy. In such cases, that part of your estate dealt with under your will goes through probate and is distributed in accordance with the terms of your will, while any parts of your estate not dealt with in your will end up going through intestate administration. This can be very costly to your estate.

Important Note

A partial intestacy occurs when the testator fails to dispose of his entire estate under his will. In such cases, property not specifically disposed of under the will generally becomes the subject of intestate administration proceedings.

Apportionment and Distribution of Assets on Intestacy

If you die intestate, the laws applicable to the distribution of your estate will be those of your state of domicile, or principal place residence. While state intestacy laws generally vary from state to state, this variance has been somewhat lessened by the Uniform Probate Code (the "Code"), which, at the time of this writing, has been adopted in full by approximately 16 states and in part by numerous others, bringing greater consistency to probate and intestacy rules. Even where your state has adopted the Code, you will still need to check your state's laws for a more sophisticated and thorough understanding of the Code as the Code often gives discretion to adopting states in relation to implementing the Code.

Uniform Probate Code - Full State Adoption

Arizona	Massachusetts	New Mexico
Colorado	Michigan	North Dakota
Hawaii	Minnesota	South Carolina
Idaho	Montana	South Dakota
Maine	Nebraska	Utah

The Code, however, does present a useful starting point for discussing intestate distribution. Under the Code, the priority of inheritance is given to the following persons in the following order:

- surviving spouse.
- descendants (children, grandchildren, etc.).
- parents.
- descendants of deceased's parents (siblings, nieces, and nephews).
- grandparents.
- descendants of grandparents (aunts and uncles and cousins).

Under the Code, relatives are each apportioned a certain percentage of the deceased's estate. The percentages are as follows:

Share of Surviving Spouse

The share of a surviving spouse is calculated as follows: -

- A surviving spouse is entitled to the entire estate if neither the deceased's descendants (i.e. children, grandchildren, and great grandchildren) nor the deceased's parents have survived the deceased.

- If the deceased's parents survive but no descendants survive the deceased, the surviving spouse is entitled to the first $200,000 of the estate plus ¾ of anything exceeding that amount.

- If the deceased is survived by a spouse and descendants from that marriage only, the surviving spouse will take the first $150,000 of the estate plus ½ of anything exceeding that amount, plus all community property.

- If the deceased is survived by descendants from the marriage to the surviving spouse and by descendants from someone other than his or her surviving spouse, the surviving spouse takes the first $100,000 of the estate plus ½ of anything exceeding that amount, plus all community property.

Share of Descendants

- If the deceased's spouse does not survive the deceased and the deceased's descendants do, then the deceased's descendants take the entire estate.

- In some cases, if the deceased's child has predeceased the deceased, that child's surviving children will inherit their parent's share of the intestate estate. This is known as 'per stirpes distribution'.

Share of Parents

- If the deceased is not survived by a spouse or descendants, his entire net estate passes to his parents equally or, if only one survives, to the survivor.

Share of Other Relatives

- If neither the deceased's spouse, descendants, nor parents survive the deceased, the entire net estate passes to the deceased's siblings. If there are no siblings or no descendants of the deceased's siblings, the deceased's estate goes to any surviving grandparents or their descendants.

If the deceased dies without a will and without traceable relatives or relatives that fall within the scope of the Code or state intestacy provisions, the estate may be transferred to the state itself under the common law of escheat.

Intestacy and Same Sex Partners

Currently, in the United States, the laws in many states do not provide a right of inheritance for surviving same-sex partners where their partner dies intestate. This generally applies irrespective of whether the partners are in a registered domestic relationship or not. While the position may change in the future, it is currently recommended that same sex partners make a will and specifically identify their partner as a beneficiary under their wills. In the absence of doing so, surviving partners may not be able to inherit from their deceased partner's estate.

There are, however, some situations in which a surviving same-sex partner can inherit from their deceased partner's estate on intestacy. For example, in California the surviving domestic partner of a same-sex couple may inherit California community property and a variable percentage of the deceased partner's separate property. The entitlement to this variable share, known as the *separate property entitlement*, will depend on whether the deceased partner was survived by children, grandchildren, parents, siblings, or other legally recognized relatives. This is similar in ways to the rules that apply to married couples of differing sexes.

It is important to realize that same-sex estate legislation may not keep pace with the granting of rights commensurate with same-sex marriage. For example, while it may be legal for couples in a same-sex partnership to now marry, that may not automatically mean that succession laws have changed to give same-sex couples the same succession rights as say married heterosexual couples or heterosexual couples in registered domestic partnership. As such, if you are in a same-sex marriage or partnership, it is important to check the laws in your state to see what succession rights you have.

Resource

The American Civil Liberties Union (the "ACLU") offers a site for legislative information for lesbian, gay and bisexual couples. It may be found at: **www.aclu.com**.

CHAPTER 4

Gifts and Beneficiaries

What is a Gift?

A gift is a voluntary transfer of property by one person to another made gratuitously, without any consideration or compensation. In a will, you may leave gifts of financial or personal value to your family and friends. Gifts come in the form of legacies, devises, and bequests. A legacy may be money, property, stocks, jewelry, or other possessions. A bequest is generally limited to personal property like jewelry, furniture, or antiques, but generally not money. Alternatively, a devise is limited to real property, like your home.

Specific Item Gifts

Specific item gifts are also known as a demonstrative legacies or bequests. These gifts include specific items of property such as a car, a piece of jewelry, stocks, bonds, and some real estate. When drafting your will, it is important to ensure that you clearly identify and describe the property that you wish to gift. For example, when gifting a car, you should describe the make, model, and color of the car rather than simply referring to "my car". This reduces the risk of confusion and accelerates the process of distributing the estate. When writing a provision for a gift, a good question to ask is whether a stranger would easily identify the gift based on the description you have included in your will.

Cash Gifts

Cash gifts are also known as monetary or pecuniary legacies. A cash gift is a gift of a specific amount of money or cash to a named beneficiary. Just as with specific item gifts, when making a cash gift it is important to clearly identify the gift you are making including the amount and currency of the gift, and the person receiving the gift. In addition, when making a cash gift, it is important to consider the financial implications of the gift on the overall estate and, in particular, whether there will be enough cash remaining in the estate to pay your debts and taxes. If not, specific assets may need to be sold to raise cash.

Residuary Gifts

The residue of estate gift (or residuary estate) is the remainder of a deceased person's estate after the payment of all debts, funeral, and testamentary expenses and after all specific item and cash gifts have been made. A residuary estate also includes property that is the subject of a failed gift. A gift fails in circumstances where the beneficiary has died or refuses to accept the gift.

The person entitled to receive a gift of the residuary estate under a will is called the residuary beneficiary or, if there is more than one residuary beneficiary, residuary beneficiaries.

A residue clause is a clause that seeks to dispose of all items of the residue of your estate. Your residuary estate can be given to one person or to a number of people in varying percentages, fractions or in sections (such as, for example, giving the remainder of your real estate in California to X, the remainder of all other real estate to Y; and the remainder of your personal property to Z).

Beneficiaries

A beneficiary is a person, organization or other entity who will inherit part of the assets or estate under your will. You are more or less free to decide who will receive your assets.

Some restrictions may be placed on minor beneficiaries, depending on the state in which you are resident. Specifically, a child will be prohibited from owning significant assets until he has reached the age of majority in his state. Where a child is named as a beneficiary under a will, the assets gifted to the child will be placed in to the care of a trustee or guardian who will hold them in trust until such time as the child is old enough to take control of the assets in his own right.

Types of Beneficiaries and Hierarchy of Distribution

There are three principal types of beneficiaries under a will. These include (1) a specific gift beneficiary, (2) an alternate beneficiary and (3) a residuary beneficiary.

Specific Gift Beneficiary

A specific gift beneficiary is a person or organization named in the will that is to receive a specific item of property from the estate. These items of property can include items such as sums of money, jewelry, and cars.

Specific gifts are generally the first gifts distributed under a will. As mentioned above, any assets that are not distributed form part of the residue of the estate and will usually be given to the person or persons named as residuary beneficiaries (unless there are taxes or other expenses to be discharged).

Alternate Beneficiary

When naming a person to receive a gift of any kind under your will, it is prudent to prepare for the possibility that he or she may be unable or unwilling to accept the gift. To this end, it is helpful to nominate an alternate beneficiary. An alternate beneficiary is a person who becomes legally entitled to inherit the gift if the first named beneficiary is unable or unwilling to accept it. A beneficiary who refuses to accept a gift is said to have 'disclaimed' their entitlement to a gift. It is advisable for your executor to have all such disclaimers in writing before the gift is passed to the alternate beneficiary. Alternate beneficiaries are the second class of beneficiaries, after the primary or first named beneficiaries, who inherit under a will.

Residuary Beneficiary

A residuary beneficiary is the person(s) or organization(s) named to receive the residue of the estate. The residue of an estate is that part of the estate which remains after the payment of all debts and expenses, and after the transfer of all specific gifts.

Restrictions on Beneficiaries

The following persons or organizations are generally precluded from receiving gifts from you under your will:

- A lawyer who was involved in drafting your will or in providing counsel to you with regards to your will. If such a lawyer was permitted to receive a gift under the terms of your will, the presumption could be raised, as a matter of law, that he exerted some form of undue influence over you which caused you to name him as a beneficiary. You can, however, appoint the lawyer as your executor and direct that he is paid for carrying out his duties as executor. If you wish to provide for a lawyer in your will, then it is advisable that you hire a third-party lawyer to draft it or draft it yourself.

- Any person who has witnessed you signing your will. This prohibition also includes the spouses of any such witnesses. This prohibition has its origins in old English rules of evidence, upon which U.S. common law is partly based. English law provided that interested parties could not testify in court as to the proper execution of a will due to their conflict of interest. As a result, most states presume that gifts to witnesses or their spouses under a will are rendered null and void. It is recommended that none of the witnesses to your will or their respective spouses, stand to benefit under your will. If you wish to leave them a gift, it's recommended that you use alternative witnesses or that you leave the gift to them under the terms of a codicil and that alternate persons witness your signing of that codicil.

- Any person who unlawfully causes your death.

- An unincorporated association that is not permitted to hold property. This is important in the context of gifts to clubs and other unincorporated organizations.

Gifts to Spouses

Before making a gift to your spouse, it is important to understand the basic differences in distribution of property in both common law property states and community property states. These differences will determine what portion of your estate (if any) you are obliged to transfer to your spouse.

Important Note

In this section, for convenience, we refer to 'spouses' only. However, the law tends to apply equally to registered domestic partners.

Community Property States

Property owned by couples in community property states is divided loosely into two categories: separate property and community property.

A spouse's separate property is all property acquired by that spouse before or after a marriage (including after a legal separation) plus all property received as a gift or an inheritance and maintained separately (not jointly owned with their spouse) during the marriage. Community property, on the other hand, is all other property earned or acquired by either spouse during a marriage.

Important Note

At the date of writing, there are nine community property states in the U.S. namely Arizona, California, Idaho, Louisiana, Nevada, New Mexico, Texas, Washington, and Wisconsin. In Alaska couples can opt to have their property treated as community property under the terms of a written property agreement. The property distribution rules in these states may also apply to registered domestic partners.

Separate property can also be deemed community property where it is formerly transferred to the joint names of both spouses. Similarly, where joint property is gifted to one spouse and commingled with community property, the property can become community property.

Alaska, Arizona, California, Nevada, Texas and Wisconsin each allow a surviving spouse to automatically inherit community property when the other spouse dies provided that the property's title document makes it clear that it is owned as community property with a 'right of survivorship' in favor of the surviving spouse.

Normally, classifying property as community or separate property is relatively straightforward.

However, there are several instances in which the classification is not clear. These include valuations of businesses, companies, pensions, the proceeds of certain lawsuits, and incomes received from separate property. In each case, you should consult a local attorney to determine how the law in your state treats these items.

Most community property states do not grant a surviving spouse a legal right to inherit from the deceased spouse's estate. Rather, community property states try to divide the marital assets during the lifetime of the spouses by classifying certain assets as community property. Each spouse in turn has a right to 50% of the community property.

However, in Alaska, California, Idaho, Washington and Wisconsin, a surviving spouse may elect to receive a specific portion of the deceased spouse's community or separate property in limited circumstances. For more information on such entitlements, we recommend that you consult a suitably qualified attorney in your state.

Important Note

If you are in a registered domestic partnership and considering a move to another state, you should pay close attention to laws of the state to which you are proposing to move as the 'new state' may not recognize the same property rights which you had in your 'old state'. If you are in any doubt as to how the law will affect you, you should consult a duly qualified attorney in your state.

Common Law States

In common law states, each spouse owns all property acquired using his or her own income as well as all property legally registered solely in his or her name. In addition, each spouse will jointly own any property, such as the marital home, that is registered in the joint names of both spouses.

Spouses in common law states will also have a legal right, known as an elective share, to a fraction of their deceased spouse's estate when he or she dies. Depending on the state in which the couple are resident when the first spouse dies, this elective share will usually be an amount equal to between one-third and one-half of the value of the deceased spouse's estate. The precise amount to which the surviving spouse is entitled will also depend on whether the couple had any minor children and whether the surviving spouse had been provided for outside the terms of the deceased spouse's will (for example, under a living trust).

The right of the surviving spouse to receive his or her elective share will take priority over any devises or legacies made in the deceased spouse's will and will rank in priority after creditors of the deceased's estate. The surviving spouse is entitled to exercise his or her right to receive the elective share or to waive that right in favor of whatever has been left to him or her under the terms of the deceased spouse's will. The entitlement to receive an elective share does not arise by operation of law. Instead, the surviving spouse must exercise the right by serving a written notice on the executor of the deceased spouse's estate within a particular time frame. If the election is not made within the required time frame, the surviving spouse is deemed to have waived any entitlement to receive his or her elective share.

In certain states, the surviving spouse may have an additional right to inherit the family home or, in certain cases, a right to live there for a defined period. In some states, the surviving spouse will even be entitled to day-to-day living expenses during the probate process.

Matters can become more complex when a couple moves from a common law state to a community property state. In California, Idaho, Washington and Wisconsin, property acquired prior to a move will be treated as if it had been acquired in the state to which the couple has moved. In other community property states, the laws stipulate that the couple's property be treated in accordance with the laws of the state in which it was acquired rather those of the community property state to which the couple has moved. The application of these rules can result in marital property being subjected to both common law and community property rules. By contrast, couples that move from a community property state to a common law state come up against the opposite problem. In such cases, each spouse usually retains a 50% interest in the community property acquired during the couple's residence in the community property state.

It is important to determine which laws affect the distribution of your property before making a will. As such, be sure to take legal advice where necessary to determine the rules applicable particularly where the rules of both community property states and common law states apply.

Gifts to Minors

Depending on each state's laws, minor children may only own a nominal amount of property in their own names, whether received under the terms of a will or otherwise. The amount varies between approximately $1,000 and $10,000 depending on the state in question. If you plan on leaving a gift to a minor in excess of the permitted statutory amount in your state, it will be necessary either by the terms of your will or by an application to court to appoint an adult called a custodian, trustee or property guardian to receive the gift on behalf of the minor. Once received, this person will manage the property on behalf of the child until the child reaches an age set out by you in your will, or an age prescribed by law.

There are three basic methods for leaving property to minor children or young beneficiaries under your will. They are as follows:

(i) Custodianship

The Uniform Transfers to Minors Act provides a mechanism by which gifts can be made to a minor without requiring the formal appointment of a guardian. Under the act, a testator can name a person in his will to act as custodian of a gift made to a young beneficiary. That custodian will receive and manage the property on behalf of the beneficiary until he or she reaches a particular age, at which time the custodianship will end, and the custodian will transfer the property to the beneficiary. While this 'age of termination' varies from state to state, it is usually between 18 to 25 years. This act has been adopted by every state in the U.S. other than South Carolina.

(ii) A Child's Trust

It is also possible to create a 'child's trust' under the terms of a will for the benefit of a child or a young adult. The will itself will provide for the creation of a trust and the transfer of some or all the testator's property to that trust upon his death. Once transferred to the trust, the trust property is ring-fenced and held separately from the property left to any other person under the testator's will. A person will be named as trustee in the will and will be responsible for the management of the trust property on behalf of the beneficiary until that beneficiary becomes entitled to receive the property in his or her own right. As the trust property is ring-fenced in the trust, it is quite common to see more than one child trust created under a will, especially where there are several young beneficiaries.

(iii) A Family Pot Trust

A family pot trust (or children's pot trust as it is sometimes referred to) is slightly different to a child's trust in that it is established for the benefit of two or more children rather than a single child. A family pot trust is managed by a trustee who will have discretion in terms of how the proceeds are distributed between each of the children. If one child needs more funds than the other, the trustee is at liberty to apply the trust funds as he sees fit.

We discuss each of these three forms of property management in more detail in Chapter 6.

Make Your Last Will Online

If you wish to create a children's pot trust, we recommend using EstateBee's Online Will Writing Software as it contains a number of flexible and complex options that cannot reasonably be catered for in 'fill-in-the-blank' type documents. You can try it for free at **www. estate-bee.com/product/online-last-will/**

Gifts to Charities

If you wish to leave a gift to a charity under your will, you should ensure that you provide clear details of the charity to be benefited. In this respect, it is useful to identity the charity by reference to its correct legal name (as it may differ from the 'trading name' commonly used by the charity) as well as its charity registration number. You should be aware that several states impose limitations on leaving large portions of your estate to charity following your death. Therefore, it is advisable to consult a lawyer if you wish to leave a large part (especially 50% or more) of your estate to one or more charitable institutions or not-for-profit organizations.

Gifts to Witnesses

Testamentary gifts and bequests made to those who witness a will are usually presumed void. As such, it is not recommended that a beneficiary named under your will or their spouse/partner act as a witness to its execution.

Failed Bequests

A gift under your will can fail if the item to be gifted is disposed of or destroyed prior to your death. Where the gift fails, the intended beneficiary will not be entitled to receive a substitute gift unless you have specified otherwise in your will. Similarly, a gift made to a person that predeceases you will also usually fail. Where it does, the gift becomes part of the residuary estate unless you have named an alternate beneficiary who is entitled to receive that gift if the first name beneficiary is unable or unwilling to receive it.

Releasing Someone from a Debt

It is possible to release or 'forgive' a debt owed to you by another person, incorporated body, or un-incorporated association under your will. Where you do so, it will legally release the debtor from the debt on your death. If you do not forgive the debt, your executor will be entitled to institute legal proceedings on behalf of your estate to recover from the debtor.

Common Disaster and Simultaneous Death

It is common in wills to insert a 'common disaster' or 'simultaneous death' provision. These provisions usually provide that in order for a beneficiary to receive a gift from you under your will, he or she must survive you for a period of time – usually 30 to 90 days following your death. These provisions help to avoid situations where the same assets are subject to several administrations in quick succession because of one or more of the beneficiaries dying within a short time of each other. They also help avoid a situation where several estates end up paying estate taxes on the same assets.

By way of illustration, consider the situation where a family of four dies in a car crash within a short time of each other. If there is no survival period, the assets of each of the family members could pass from their estate to that of one of the other family members immediately upon their death. If the recipient dies shortly afterwards, his assets will pass to the next family member, and so on. The common disaster provision avoids this by stipulating that a person shall not be entitled to receive an asset from the deceased's estate unless he survives the deceased by a particular period. If he does not survive the deceased for the required time, he is deemed to have died before the deceased and the deceased's assets will pass to another surviving beneficiary or heir rather than to him.

Common disaster provisions are often used between spouses who agree to pass their estate to the other spouse if they survive, or to their children or a third party if not.

Disinheritance

While the laws vary from state to state, the only people that generally have a right to inherit from your estate are your spouse, children, and grandchildren. However, it is possible to disinherit your children intentionally or unintentionally and, to a lesser extent, your spouse in most states. You can intentionally disinherit your children by intentionally failing to name them in your will or by making a nominal gift to them. You can also unintentionally disinherit children by accidentally failing to mention them in your will. Spouses are a little harder to disinherit because of their entitlement to an elective share of your estate but you can construct your will so that they only receive the minimum entitlement that the law affords them. Of course, if you try to disinherit family members, they may challenge the terms of your will in court. The success of any such claims would ultimately depend on the laws of your state, the claimant in question and the circumstances surrounding the disinheritance. If you wish to disinherit a family member, speak to an attorney.

Disinheriting Your Spouse

As already mentioned, in most states you cannot simply disinherit your spouse. If you live in a community property state, then your spouse is generally entitled to half of your community property. On the other hand, if you live in a common law state, the law allows spouses to legally claim up to half of your estate regardless of the terms of your will. It is, therefore, quite difficult to disinherit a spouse from his or her full legal entitlement – although you can leave them with less than your entire estate.

Disinheriting Your Child

By contrast to spouses, and much unlike the laws in other common law countries, it is possible to completely disinherit children in virtually every state in the U.S. In order to disinherit a child, your will must either (i) expressly state that you intend to disinherit your child or (ii) make only a nominal gift to the child (such as a gift of $10, for example). If you fail to adopt either of these two approaches and simply fail to mention your child in your will, then you will run the risk of a court making a determination that there was an accidental disinheritance. In which case, the court could order a re-distribution of your estate to include a share for the omitted child.

In some states, the disinheritance laws apply not only to children but also to grandchildren. Where it does apply, grandchildren can challenge the will of a deceased grandparent who failed to provide for them or for their dead parent. As such, it is important to ensure that grandchildren are expressly disinherited in the same way as children if it is in fact your intention to disinherit both sets of descendants.

In certain circumstances, children are entitled to claim a share of a deceased parent's property, regardless of the terms of their parent's will. For example, if you live in the state of Florida and are the head of your family for tax purposes, you will be prohibited from leaving your home under your will to anyone other than your spouse or children.

If you have a child born after your will is made, then it will be necessary for you to make a new will or a codicil to the existing will in order to disinherit that child even where your existing will already states that you wish to disinherit all of your children. This is because it will be presumed that you only intended to disinherit your children who were alive at the time you made your will and not those born afterwards.

If you plan on disinheriting a child, be sure to check the applicable laws in your state.

No Contest Clauses

If you wish to disinherit a child, in whole or in part, your intention to do so should be clearly stated in your will and a no-contest clause should be included. If you do this, you should effectively disinherit that child. A 'no-contest' clause is a clause in a will that is designed to disinherit a beneficiary of a will in full if that beneficiary challenges the terms of the will in court. Where the beneficiary challenges the will, or any provision in it, the clause triggers what is virtually a complete and total disinheritance of the beneficiary. An example of a simple 'no contest' clause is set out below:

> "If any person, whether or not related to me by blood or in any way, shall attempt, either directly or indirectly, to set aside the probate of my will or oppose or contest any of the provisions hereof, then any share or interest in my estate given to that person under my will shall be revoked and, in its stead, I give and bequeath the sum of one dollar ($1.00), only that, and no further interest whatever in my estate to such person."

The Uniform Probate Code allows for the enforcement of no-contest clauses so long as the person challenging the will doesn't have probable cause to do so (i.e. where the will has been fraudulently altered, for example).

Challenging a Will

A 'will contest' or 'will challenge' is a legal objection to a will that is usually initiated by a family member or close relative of the deceased who feels cheated out of their rightful inheritance and wishes to challenge the validity of the will in court.

Challenges to a will typically focus on the following assertions:

- that the testator lacked sufficient mental capacity to fully understand what he was doing in making the will.
- that the testator was subjected to undue influence from a family member or advisor.
- that the will has been fraudulently tampered with.
- that the will has not been properly executed or witnessed in accordance with the law.
- that the challenger has not been properly provided for under the terms of the will.

Reducing Potential Challenges to a Will

The very act of making a will is often sufficient to create rifts and fighting between family members. If you suspect that your family members might challenge your will there are several steps that you can take to alleviate some of the possibilities of that claim being successful.

First and foremost, make an appointment to see your lawyer. You should ask your lawyer to review your will and any other estate planning documents that you have created. Following that review, you can discuss and agree with the lawyer whether any changes need to be made to these documents in order to better protect your distribution plan having regard to your specific circumstances and the specific threats that you envisage. An experienced estate-planning lawyer can answer questions about your will as well as questions regarding potential challenges to your will, living trust, power of attorney or healthcare directive. Your lawyer should be able to identify whether your estate plan will hold up under the challenges of your relatives.

Second, where you intend to disinherit a child or spouse, make sure you adhere to the guidelines set out above in relation to disinheriting family members.

Third, make sure that you sign your will in the presence of two witnesses (or three in Vermont) and, even if your state does not require it, consider having your witnesses sign in front of a notary. Given that the witnesses themselves sign a statement to the effect that you appeared to know and understand what you were signing and that you did so voluntarily, later challenges to your competency will be extremely difficult.

Finally, you should also consider getting a doctor's statement in or around the same time as you sign your will. The doctor should be able to provide a dated statement to the effect that he or she met you on the date in question and that, in their professional opinion, you were mentally aware and of sound mind. You can attach this statement to the back of your will as an addendum if you wish. This will help avoid challenges to your will on the grounds that you lacked the mental capacity to legally make it.

CHAPTER 5

Appointing Executors

Appointing an Executor

An executor is an individual who is charged with settling or winding up the estate of a deceased person in accordance with the terms of their will. In your will, you will need to nominate someone to carry out this role. If you die without a valid will, then this person will be appointed by the probate court and will be known as the administrator of your estate.

Your executor can be a relative, a lawyer or even a beneficiary under your will. You can even appoint more than one executor if you wish. Where more than one executor is appointed, co-executors can act separately (each one with full authority) or they can be required to act jointly, in which case both (or all if there are more than two) executors must agree to a course of action before taking that action.

Did You Know

In these states, executors are more commonly referred to as "personal representatives":

Alaska	Maine	North Dakota
Arizona	Michigan	South Carolina
Colorado	Minnesota	South Dakota
Florida	Montana	Utah
Hawaii	Nebraska	Wisconsin
Idaho	New Mexico	

Alternate Executors

When making a will, it is recommended that you appoint one or more alternate executors. An alternate executor is someone who will perform the duties of the primary executor if he is unable or unwilling to act as executor of your estate. If your alternate executor is required to act, he or she will be bound by the same fiduciary duties and responsibilities as the original primary executor.

Overview of Executors' Duties

Once formally appointed by the probate court, your executor will have the legal and fiduciary duty to safeguard, manage and distribute your estate in accordance with the terms of your will. He will also be responsible for ensuring that your estate pays any debts or taxes owing by you at the time of your death. These debts and taxes, if any, will normally need to be paid before your estate can be distributed to the beneficiaries named in your will.

Your executor's main duties will include:

- collecting, assessing, and managing your assets.

- assessing and paying your debts (including your funeral bill and the costs of probate) and taxes.

- making cash gifts, bequests, and transfers of real and personal property from your estate in accordance with the terms of your will.

Your executor will also be required to report your death, within any applicable time frames, to insurance companies, banks and other institutions that may owe money to your estate following your death.

If a trust is established under your will for the benefit of certain beneficiaries, your executor may also be required to act as trustee of that trust – unless of course other trustees are named in your will. As trustee, the executor will be responsible for protecting, preserving and investing the trust assets until the time comes to vest them in the beneficiaries, when they come of age, or at a time you have designated in your will. Trustees are often empowered, particularly where a trust is established for the benefit a child, to draw funds from the trust and apply them towards the maintenance, education and welfare of the beneficiaries until they are entitled to receive the main corpus (body) of the trust.

The duties of an executor will continue until all debts and taxes have been paid and all assets of the estate distributed. Thereafter, the estate can be would up and the executor can be released from office.

Getting Started - Locating Your Will

Before the probate of your estate begins, your executor will first need to locate your will. Not alone does your will set out how you want your estate divided, but it also identifies the person who you have nominated to act as your executor. As such, it is generally recommended that you provide your executor with a copy of your will or, at the very least, tell him where it can be found when the time comes.

Once located, your executor will need to carry out some basic checks on your will to determine whether it is valid. First, he will need to check that it has been properly signed by you and witnessed by the correct number of people. As you will remember from earlier chapters, the laws in most states require that a will be witnessed by two witnesses. Next, he will need to confirm that the will is in fact your 'last' will and testament as only your last will has any legal effect. To do this, he will need to check the date of the will and ensure that the will includes language revoking all earlier wills and codicils that you may have made. For practical reasons, and to avoid ambiguity, it is generally recommended that you destroy your old will immediately upon signing a new one.

If it turns out that the will is invalid, then your proposed executor should proceed as if you died intestate.

Applying for Probate

Assuming that your will is in order, the next steps for your executor will be to determine whether probate is required and, if so, apply for a grant of probate (often referred to as letters). Whether or not probate is required usually depends on the net value of your estate at the time of your death. If that value is less than the amount prescribed by state law, probate may not be required. Alternatively, if your estate is deemed to be a 'small estate' because of its low financial value, your executor may be entitled to avail of an informal streamlined probate procedure. However, if the value of the estate exceeds the relevant financial threshold, formal probate may be required.

Where formal probate is required, your executor will need to apply for a grant of probate. He will do this by submitting an original copy of your will and a certified copy of your death certificate to the probate court. In conjunction with that, he will need to notify certain interested parties (including your heirs and persons named in your will) that he has formally applied to be appointed as executor of your estate. If any of the interested parties wish to object to his appointment, or indeed challenge the terms of your will, they will be required to make those objections and/or challenges within the relevant time frame set out in the notice, as prescribed under state law. Failing which, the court will make a ruling on the validity of your will and appoint the person you have nominated in your will as executor (unless it has good reason not to).

Contrary to what you might see on TV, formal court appearances before a probate judge are relatively rare. In fact, in most cases, the probate process is an administrative one carried out by your executor with assistance from the probate court clerk and the estate's lawyers (if any). Occasionally, meetings may be held with a judge in chambers or in a court building conference room to discuss problems relating to the administration of the estate. Beyond that, however, the process is very much limited to the making of filings and the serving of notices.

Administering the Estate

Once the court deems your will to be valid, and accepts your nomination of executor, it will formally appoint your chosen person as executor of your estate. It will also issue letters of authority to your executor. These letters evidence his formal appointment as executor and permit him to represent the estate to third parties.

Your executor will then begin the process of reviewing your personal records and affairs, locating, and safeguarding assets, paying taxes, settling debts and formulating a plan for distributing your estate.

For more information on probating an estate, see our book entitled "How to Probate an Estate - A Step-By-Step Guide for Executors".

Resource

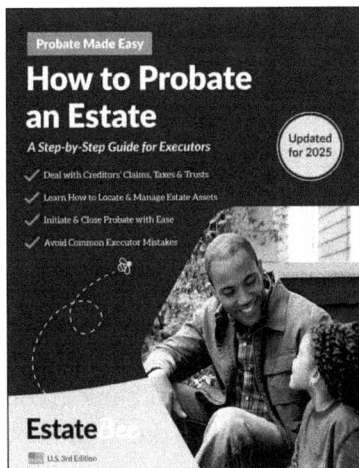

"How to Probate an Estate" is essential reading for anyone thinking about acting as an executor of someone's estate. It is designed to guide readers step-by-step through the entire probate process and to give them the knowledge and confidence to act as an executor.

It explores each step of the probate process from the moment the deceased dies right through to the distribution of the deceased's assets and the closing of the estate. It is a one-stop resource for successfully probating an estate.

Get your copy at
www.estate-bee.com/product/how-to-probate-an-estate/

Closing the Estate

Once your executor has dealt with the administration of the estate, the next step in the process will be to prepare and finalize the documents required for closing the estate. In this respect, your executor will need to prepare (or have an accountant do so) an accounting setting out details of the transactions that have taken place in relation to the estate. Your executor will need to file that accounting with the probate court together with (i) evidence that all taxes owing by the estate have been paid and (ii) a plan as to how the estate will be distributed (if it hasn't already been distributed pre-closing). Where the estate has already been distributed in part or in whole, your executor may need to provide evidence of those distributions to the court. That evidence will usually take the form of receipts signed by the beneficiaries or copies of deeds signed by the executor in connection with the transfer of real and personal property. Once the court reviews the paperwork and is satisfied that your executor has successfully administered your estate, it will issue an order releasing him from further service as executor.

The steps above relating to probate are broadly like those that an administrator would need to carry out in relation to the administration of an estate.

Providing for Your Family During Probate

During the probate process, most of your assets will be frozen. However, if you plan ahead, there are a number of ways in which your family can have access to funds to meet their short-term needs. For immediate funds for living expenses, your family can turn to assets that fall outside of the probate estate. These assets are not frozen by probate and usually include insurance proceeds that are payable to your family on death; assets held in a living trust; joint bank accounts; pay-on-death accounts; property held in joint tenancy; or assets passing to a designated beneficiary outside of probate on your death.

Most states also do their part in providing for the family's needs, often by providing financial assistance for the surviving spouse and minor children. This financial assistance comes in the form of 'homestead rights'. This is a right given to the family upon your death to remain in and occupy the family home for a period of time - even in the case where the home has been left to someone else under your will. There are also other similar rights that your family will be entitled to receive – including rights to automobiles, a certain amount of estate property, etc. You should check the laws of your state to determine what specific rights your family might have. This will help you in creating an overall estate plan that achieves your goals.

Who can be an Executor?

In most states, any person over the age of 18 who has not been convicted of a felony may become an executor. That said, there are some restrictions on appointing out-of-state executors.

Naming an Out-of-State Executor

While you are not directly prohibited from naming an out-of-state executor, your state may impose some restrictions on appointing such executors. For example, in certain states, out-of-state executors are required to be either relatives or beneficiaries of the testator. Other states require a non-residential executor to post a bond to ensure that the beneficiaries under your will are protected against potential wrongdoings by this executor. The laws in some states permit the testator to waive this requirement by making appropriate provisions in his will, yet the laws in other states prohibit such waivers.

Bonds, while paid for by the estate, can be expensive. As such, depending on the applicable laws, it may make sense to appoint an executor who lives in your state of residence. This might make it easier and cheaper in the long run.

Choosing an Executor

Choosing an executor is one of the most fundamental elements of any will. The main characteristics of a good executor are good common sense, excellent organizational skills, and integrity. Some people choose to appoint their spouse, a sibling, or an adult child, while others prefer to nominate a professional such as a lawyer or accountant. Alternatively, it can simply be a good friend. Whoever you choose should be both competent and trustworthy.

It will often pay to choose a family member or friend as executor for the simple reason that these people expect little – if any – compensation for the job, will respect your wishes, and are generally keen to process things and finalize them as soon as possible. However, keep in mind that the process can be quite administrative, and time is often of the essence. You must choose someone who is organizationally reliable. It also makes sense to appoint someone who is living nearby as an executor so that they will be well placed to deal with the management, collection, and distribution of the estate's assets.

The executor must be willing and prepared to carry out all the legal steps required by state law to finalize your estate. So do consult your proposed executor before nominating him to ensure that he would be happy to take on the role. If the job is likely to be a sizeable one, it is common for executors to be paid fees out of the estate to compensate them for their services. Executor fees are often statutorily limited to a percentage of the estate value or as 'reasonable compensation'. However, often only professional executors require payment.

CHAPTER 6

Guardians and Children

Guardians

A guardian is the person responsible for a child's (or other dependent or incapacitated person's) physical care, education, health, and welfare, as well as for making decisions about a child's faith-related matters. In some states, a non-parent guardian is called a 'conservator'.

Normally, parents are the primary legal guardians of their minor children - including both adopted children and those born of a marriage. If one parent dies, the other becomes the sole guardian of the children. However, if the sole surviving parent passes without making proper provision for the care of his or her children, those children could become the responsibility of the state. In which case, they could be placed with a family relative chosen by the court, in foster care or otherwise. To avoid such a situation occurring, it's important that you plan ahead and ensure that a proper plan is in place to care for your children if neither you nor the other parent of the children is around to take care of them.

The only means by which you can have control over the care of your children after you die is by making suitable provision for the appointment of a guardian for those children. This can be done under the terms of a guardianship agreement or under your will. It is also generally recommended that, when you appoint a guardian, you also appoint an alternate guardian who will be asked to care for your children in the event that the primary guardian is unable or unwilling to do so.

Sole and Joint Guardians

You may appoint one or more guardians to care for the children. One guardian is known as a sole guardian and is solely responsible for the children and for making all decisions on their behalf. Nominating two or more persons means they serve together as joint guardians to the children. Given that joint guardians must reach agreement in relation to all decisions regarding the children in their care, joint-guardians are usually nominated only when they are married to each other or live together, as well as where they each have important relationships with the children (uncles or aunts, for example).

If you are considering appointing a married couple as joint guardians, be sure to carefully consider the status of the married couple's relationship and whether you would want both spouses to serve if they were separated or divorced. In such an instance, it may be preferable to simply appoint one spouse as the guardian.

Alternate Guardians

Naming alternate guardians is recommended because it provides an alternative if the named guardian in the will becomes unable to fulfill that role. As with joint guardians, alternate guardians can serve alone or jointly with a joint guardian.

Appointment of a Guardian

Using simple legal documents, such as a last will and testament or a guardianship agreement, you can nominate a trusted guardian who respects your values to look after your children after you die. However, the mere act of naming a person in your will to act as guardian of your children does not guarantee that he or she will be appointed as their legal guardian. That decision rests with a court sitting in the state in which you are resident. In such instances, the judge will honor your request to the extent he can having regard to what he believes to be in the best interests of the children. If he believes that the interests of the children are better served by placing them under the guardianship of another person, he will have full liberty to make that determination.

Important Note

As well as being able to nominate a guardian under your will, you can also nominate a guardian under the terms of a written guardianship agreement between you (as parent) and the proposed guardian. Guardianship agreements tend to go into a lot more detail regarding the guardianship arrangement than wills – which tent to merely deal with the nomination of the proposed guardian.

You may also nominate different guardians to look after different interests of your children, e.g. financial, educational, spiritual, etc. In this way, you can choose to provide for your children by ensuring that they have access to the best aspects of each of their guardians.

Who can be a Guardian?

In brief, anyone can be a guardian if they are willing and able to act as a guardian to the children and are over the age of majority.

Things to Consider When Choosing a Guardian

The decision as to whom you should nominate as a guardian is an extremely important one, and one that should not be made lightly. It is important to choose a person that will offer the best care and support to your children. Often this will be a close relative or family friend. However, before nominating a person, ask whether they are willing to accept the responsibilities that come with the role.

Important Tip

Discuss your choice with the person(s) you have selected and make sure he or she (or they) is willing to accept the responsibility of caring for your children.

There are many issues to consider when deciding whether a person would be the right person to appoint as a guardian for your children, including but not limited to the following:

- Is the person you are considering willing to accept the long-term responsibility of being a guardian?

- Is this person responsible and capable of the task of raising your children?

- Is the person an adult? A minor cannot act as a legal guardian for another minor.

- Does the person reside within a reasonable distance from the child's current home, family, friends, and school?

- Would the children be uprooted if they went to live with this guardian? Would that be in their best interests?

- Naming the same guardian for each of the minor children. Generally, courts do not like to separate siblings when determining guardianship.

- What is this person's domestic status? For example, does he or she have a house or a one-bed apartment? Is the potential guardian in a stable relationship?

- Will the potential guardian be able to provide your children with a stable positive environment and home life?

- Will your children still have easy access to their other relatives?

- What are the proposed guardian's religious and moral beliefs?

- Does he or she have any medical conditions or other issues that would prevent him/her from being a suitable guardian?

- Will this person be able to afford to care for your children?

Once you have selected someone to act as a guardian to your children, it is important to discuss the potential appointment with him. Some individuals will be unable or unwilling to accept the responsibility of being a guardian. Also, be wary of people agreeing to accept the role insincerely in the expectation that they will never be called upon to act. In fact, this is another particularly good reason to appoint an alternate guardian.

As mentioned above, naming a guardian in a will is merely a nomination, not an actual appointment. A court will still need to approve the appointment of the guardian(s). In the normal course, the court will usually ratify the appointment of a person nominated in a will unless it finds compelling reasons not to do so. However, it is always possible that interested family members or other parties may challenge the appointment. If this happens, the court will listen to all relevant parties before making a determination as to whether the nomination should stand or whether it would be in the best interest of the children to have another person appointed as guardian. The court is concerned primarily with the best interests of the children.

Given the requirement for court approval and the potential for challenges, it is recommended that where you nominate a guardian you also specify, either in your will or on a separate document, the reasons for nominating the guardian in question. This will have a strong persuasive effect when being considered by the court.

If you are not married to the other parent of your minor child, it is important to understand that the nomination of a guardian in your will does not of itself grant priority to your guardian over the rights of the surviving parent. In most cases, the surviving parent's rights will take priority over the rights of the nominated guardian.

Absence of a Guardian

If you do not' name a guardian for your minor children in your will or elsewhere in a legal document, the decision to appoint a guardian will fall to the courts. Probate courts usually give preference to family members based on the family member's relationship to the child. Generally, the court unsurprisingly decides that the child's other parent is best placed to care for the child.

However, if you are separated or divorced, you may not want your child's other parent to have custodial or guardianship rights over your child. This may be because you feel that the other parent is incapable of properly caring for the child. If you find yourself in such a position, contact an attorney or legal aid service, which will advise you appropriately and may even put in place a separate court approved guardianship agreement for the child. A court may grant custody to someone other than a surviving parent where it is satisfied that the surviving parent has legally abandoned the child or that the surviving parent is unfit or unsuitable to properly care for the child.

Where the other parent is not willing to care for the child or is deemed to be unsuitable, the court will look next to the child's grandparents, aunts or uncles, adult siblings or other relatives to see if they would be suitable guardians. A court will not know your children or your wishes for them. As such, if you believe that any of these relatives would be unsuitable, you should visit a suitably qualified attorney to make legal arrangements for someone else to care for your children should the need arise.

Important Tip

If you are concerned that a relative might legally challenge your choice of guardian for your children, we recommend that you contact a suitably qualified attorney to discuss your situation.

Children's Inheritances & Property Guardians

Children under the age of majority lack sufficient legal capacity to receive and manage inherited property. While this lack of capacity is often not an issue for most minors, it can become a problem when they inherit significant or valuable assets. In such cases, it becomes necessary to appoint an adult called a custodian, trustee, or property guardian to receive and manage the property on their behalf.

A property guardian will have full responsibility for the management of property left to a child under his care. He will be required to manage that property in the best interests of the child and, where appropriate, apply it towards the child's normal living expenses, as well as his or her health and educational needs.

While a property guardian can be appointed under the terms of a will, the scope of his management authority extends beyond the management of property left to a child under that will. In fact, it extends to include any property later received by that child in circumstances where no arrangements (whether under the terms of a trust or otherwise) have been made for the management of that property on his or her behalf. By way of illustration, if the child receives an inheritance from a long lost relative, his or her property guardian will be authorized to manage that property on behalf of the child if the relative has not provided for a specific means of managing it.

Failing to Designate a Property Guardian

If you fail to nominate a property guardian under your will, whether for your children or another minor beneficiary, the court will do so for you by appointing a person of its choosing to act as the child's property guardian. Like normal guardians, a court will often appoint the surviving parent, but this is not always the case. A third party or court appointed guardian can be appointed to manage the property on behalf of the minor and, in such cases, that property guardian will have complete control over the minor's inheritance. It follows that if you want to retain control over the appointment, it is important that you nominate a property guardian in your will or in another legal document.

Uniform Transfer to Minors' Act

Minors in most states do not have the legal capacity to enter legal contracts and are therefore not in a position to own and manage stocks, bonds, funds, life insurances and other annuities. As a result, it is important to recognize that you cannot simply transfer any of these items directly to minor children.

One of the most common methods of getting around this problem is to create a trust. Upon the testator's death, and provided the relevant terms are included in his will, a trust would be automatically created for the benefit of a named child beneficiary. Simultaneously with the creation of that trust, the assets left by the testator to the child would be transferred into the trust, to be held and managed by the trustee for the benefit of the child. During the term of the trust, the trustee would usually have discretion to provide for the child's needs and welfare from the trust fund (resulting in a depletion of the balance of the trust fund over time). Once the child reached the age of legal majority in his state or a specific age set out in the will (known as the age of termination), the trust would automatically terminate and the balance of the trust property would be transferred to the child free from the provisions of the trust.

Trusts were however often perceived as complicated and expensive to set up. Fortunately, the Uniform Gift to Minors Act ("UMGA") sought to end this by creating a simple way for assets to be transferred to minors without the need for lawyers, complicated testamentary trusts, and the associated legal costs. It operated by allowing a testator to simply gift property to a custodian (like a trustee) named in his will to be held by that custodian until the child was of sufficient age to receive the inheritance. In much the same way as a trust set out what a trustee could and couldn't do, and what he should do, the UGMA did much the same for custodians thereby creating a simple framework for creating trusts or 'custodianships'.

The UGMA was repealed in large part by the Uniform Transfer to Minors Act ("UTMA"). The UTMA, while similar in its approach to the UGMA, is widely considered to be more flexible. This is because it also applies to property received by inheritance rather than only to property received by means of a gift from a living person; and because it allowed minors to receive additional types of property such as real estate, patents and royalties. .

In order to set up a custodianship, all you need to do is identify the property that you wish to gift, the name of the child you wish to make the gift to and the name of person who will act as the child's custodian. Then simply gift the property to the custodian to hold on behalf of the child until he is old enough to receive the gift. A typical clause of this type would be written something like this: -

> *"I give $25,000 to James Jones, as custodian for Sarah Parker under the California Uniform Transfers to Minors Act."*

As mentioned, the age of termination is the statutory age at which a minor becomes legally entitled to call for the assets held by a custodian under the UTMA to be transferred to him and to have the custodial trust terminated. The table below shows the age which minors must reach in each state before a custodial trust created in that state can terminate. Where a range of ages is provided, the testator will be entitled to choose an age from that range at which the custodial trust will terminate.

The age of termination in a particular state is not always the same as the age of majority in that state. The age of majority for each state is listed in the table in Chapter 2 above.

State	UGMA	UTMA	UGMA Repeal *
Alabama	19	21	October 1, 1986
Alaska	18	18-25	January 1, 1991
Arizona	18	21	September 30, 1988

Arkansas	21	18-21	March 21, 1985
California	18	18-25	January 1, 1985
Colorado	21	21	July 1, 1984
Connecticut	21	21	October 1, 1995
Delaware	18	21	June 26, 1996
District of Columbia	18	18-21	March 12, 1986
Florida	18	21-25*	October 1, 1985
Georgia	21	21	July 1, 1990
Guam	21	N/A	N/A
Hawaii	18	21	July 1, 1985
Idaho	18	21	July 1, 1984
Illinois	21	21	July 1, 1986
Indiana	18	21	July 1, 1989
Iowa	21	21	July 1, 1986
Kansas	18	21	July 1, 1985
Kentucky	21	18	July 15, 1986
Louisiana	18	18	January 1, 1988
Maine	21	18-21	August 4, 1988
Maryland	18	21	July 1, 1989
Massachusetts	18	21	January 30, 1987
Michigan	18	18-21	December 29, 1999
Minnesota	18	21	January 1, 1986

Mississippi	21	21	January 1, 1995
Missouri	21	21	September 28, 1985
Montana	18	21	October 1, 1985
Nebraska	19	21	July 15, 1992
Nevada	18	18-25	July 1, 1985
New Hampshire	21	21	July 30, 1985
New Jersey	21	18-21	July 1, 1987
New Mexico	21	21	July 1, 1989
New York	18	21	July 10, 1996
North Carolina	18	18-21	October 1, 1987
North Dakota	18	21	July 1, 1985
Ohio	18	21-25	May 7, 1986
Oklahoma	21	18-21	November 1, 1986
Oregon	21	21-25	January 1, 1986
Pennsylvania	21	21-25	December 16, 1992
Rhode Island	21	21	July 23, 1998
South Carolina	18	21	June 17, 2022
South Dakota	18	18	July 1, 1986
Tennessee	18	21-25	October 1, 1992
Texas	18	21	September 1, 1995
Utah	21	21	July 1, 1990
Vermont	18	21	January 15, 2003

Virgin Islands	21	N/A	N/A
Virginia	18	18-21, or 25	July 1, 1988
Washington	21	21 or 25	July 1, 1991
West Virginia	18	21	July 1, 1986
Wisconsin	18	21	April 8, 1988
Wyoming	18	21-30	May 22, 1987

*   In Florida, a UTMA custodianship can be established to terminate when a beneficiary reaches an age between 21 and 25. However, if the selected age is beyond 21, the custodian must allow the beneficiary the option to terminate the custodianship and take full control of the assets within 30 days after their 21st birthday. This means that even if you plan for the custodianship to end at, say, age 23, the beneficiary has the right to access the assets earlier if they choose. To prevent this scenario, consider using a child's trust or consult a qualified Florida estate planning attorney for tailored advice.

**   While most states replaced the UGMA with UTMA, not all did. Trusts created in these states will therefore continue to use the age of termination referenced in the UGMA. Similarly, trusts created in states which adopted the UTMA before the adoption date will, in many cases, continue to use the UGMA age as the relevant age of termination for those trusts.

Child Trusts

A child's trust is valid in all U.S. states and can be created under the terms of a will – such trusts are often called testamentary trusts. A trust is a fiduciary arrangement whereby the testator appoints one or more persons to become the legal owners of trust property, which they hold for the benefit of another person – a child or young beneficiary in this case.

To create a child's trust under your will, you will need to provide for the creation of that trust in your will using certain required legal language. You will also need to name the person who will act as trustee of that trust, the child or young beneficiary who will be entitled to receive the assets held in that trust and the age at which he will be entitled to do so – which can be any age above the age of majority (although 18 – 25 years is the norm). If the child is already over this age at the time of your death, and has reached the age of majority in his state, the trust will never actually come into existence and the property will instead be transferred directly to the child upon your death.

On the other hand, if the proposed child beneficiary is under the trust's age of termination at the time of your death, the trust will be created and the relevant property will be deemed to have been transferred into the trust fund. Thereafter, the trust assets will be managed by the trustee in accordance with provisions set out in your will. The trustee will manage those assets until the child beneficiary has reached the age specified in your will. At that time, the remainder of the assets will be transferred to him and the trust will be terminated.

During the trust, the trustee will have broad discretion over the management and distribution of the trust assets. If the trustee deems it appropriate, monies can usually be released to the child from time to time to cover matters ranging from education to medical treatment to general maintenance.

While court supervision is generally not required with these types of trusts, serving as a trustee can be more onerous than simply serving as a custodian under the UTMA. For example, a trustee is required to file annual income tax returns for the trust with the IRS. Also, as the powers of trustees of testamentary trusts are set out in the will itself, it will be necessary for the trustee to produce copies of the will every time he has to deal with a financial institution on behalf of the trust's beneficiary. In which cases, queries may be raised as to how the trust operates, the authority of the trustee, and so on. By contrast, given that the powers of a UTMA custodian are provided under statute, most banks and other financial institutions are more familiar with their terms and more knowledgeable of the authority given to custodians under these statutes. This allows for a much easier level of interaction with the financial institutions.

Children's and Family Pot Trusts

A pot trust is a good tool to use with younger children as it allows you to place monies in trust to benefit two or more children. They are somewhat unique in that the trust assets can be made available to whichever child needs them the most rather than being divided equally for the benefit of each child beneficiary. In this regard, the trustee has discretion to apportion the trust fund between the children as he or she sees fit. For example, if one of your children wishes to go to college, your trustee can take a portion of the money from the trust to send that child to college. Similarly, should one of your children require an expensive medical treatment, monies can be released from the trust to cover the costs of the treatment.

A pot trust will terminate when the youngest child reaches a specific age determined by the will which is usually an age between 18 to 25 years. At that time, the trust is divided between the children equally. One of the principal drawbacks to using a pot trust is, however, that older children cannot receive their share of the trust property until the youngest child reaches the designated age of termination. As such, in certain cases, some of the beneficiaries could be well into adulthood by the time they receive their share of the inheritance.

Choosing a Trustee

A trustee's duties can continue for several years and, in many cases, require expertise in investing money, dealing with real estate, paying bills, filing accounts, and managing money on behalf of the trust's underlying beneficiaries.

In practice, most people who establish a trust choose a family member as trustee because family members tend not to charge fees for acting as trustee. This is fine so long as the family member is capable of handling financial matters competently and has sufficient time to carry out his role.

Professional trustees will charge annual management fees for acting as trustees. In some instances, these fees can be significant. However, given the expertise that a professional trustee can bring to the table, it is important to at least consider engaging a professional where you have a large estate.

If you decide not to proceed with a professional trustee, then the characteristics you should consider in appointing an individual trustee are much the same as those you look for in an executor.

Trustee's Duties

Trustees have many duties. A trustee occupies a fiduciary position (a position of trust) and is therefore bound to act for the benefit of and in the best interests of another. Some specific duties of trustees include the following:

- **The Duty to Adhere to the Terms of the Trust**

  Trustees are required to administer a trust according to its terms. Surprisingly, however, trustees' decisions are often made without referring to the trust provisions to establish whether the act in question is permitted under the terms of the trust. This can have adverse effects on the value of the underlying trust assets and expose the trustee to personal liability.

- **The Duty to Act Personally**

  Unless the trust terms permit otherwise, trustees must act personally and may not delegate the performance of tasks or the making of decisions concerning the trust to others – although the trustee is normally permitted to take legal and other professional advice when necessary.

- **The Duty to Act in the Best Interests of the Beneficiaries**

  The trustee is required to act impartially and in the best interest of the trust's beneficiaries. If he does not, a beneficiary can apply to the court to have him removed or to have his decision reviewed or reversed.

- **The Duty to Account**

  Trustees are required to keep full and proper financial records for the trust – including an accounting of all transactions carried out by the trust and all distributions and returns made by it.

- **The Duty to Supply Information**

  A trust's beneficiaries are entitled to certain information regarding the trust. This information usually includes a copy of the trust deed, a copy of the latest financial accounts, copies of title documents relating to trust assets and details of distributions made from the trust to beneficiaries. However, while being required to provide information, trustees are not normally required to provide explanations for their decisions, minutes of trustee meetings (if any), copies of correspondence between trustees and beneficiaries, nor a copy of any memorandum of wishes provided by the testator.

- **The Duty to Invest Prudently**

  Trustees are required to exercise the due care, diligence, and skill that a reasonable prudent person would exercise in managing the affairs of others.

- **The Duty to Carry Out Duties Without Payment**

  Other than out of pocket expenses, trustees are generally required to act without payment unless the trust terms provide otherwise. Professional trustees will always charge fees and will always ensure that a power to pay them is contained in the trust provisions before they act.

- **The Duty to Not Benefit Personally from the Trust**

  As a fiduciary, a trustee may not personally benefit unless the trust deed specifically allows for this.

- **Duty to Avoid Conflicts of Interest**

  Trustees are required to act in good faith and to avoid conflicts of interest. When a conflict of interest arises, a trustee should act carefully and consider taking professional advice.

CHAPTER 7

Estate Planning

Overview of Estate Planning

Estate planning is the process of planning for the management and distribution of your estate in the event of your incapacity or death. It is also one of the most important means by which you can ensure that your personal healthcare preferences are honored if you become incapacitated and unable to communicate your wishes to attending physicians.

A comprehensive estate plan will include relevant legal devices to transfer property, appoint guardians for children, reduce tax, avoid probate, provide for the management of financial affairs, and make healthcare decisions and funeral arrangements. Regardless of a person's age or the size of their estate, a good estate plan can accomplish each of these tasks for them.

Understanding estate planning options can appear to be quite a demanding endeavor at first glance. However, many of the estate planning techniques commonly used are in fact relatively easy to understand and straightforward to use. In the ensuing pages, we will introduce you to some of the most common techniques.

Resource

Estate Planning
Essentials

A step-by-step guide to estate planning

Includes
Estate Planning
Worksheets

✓ Prepare an effective estate plan
✓ Provide for children & other beneficiaries
✓ Plan for medical incapacity
✓ Save on legal fees & taxes

Estate

U.S. 3rd Edition

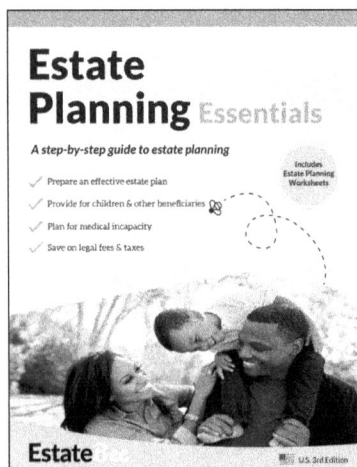

"Estate Planning Essentials" is a must read for anyone who doesn't already have a comprehensive estate plan. It will show you the importance of having wills, trusts, powers of attorney and living wills in your estate plan. You will learn about the probate process, why people are so keen to avoid it and lots of simple methods you can use to do so. You will also learn about reducing estate taxes and how best to provide for young beneficiaries and children.

This book is a great way to get you started on the way to making your own estate plan. Get your copy at

www.estate-bee.com/product/estate-planning-essentials/

Last Will and Testament

Aside from facilitating the transfer of property to loved ones following death, a will is extremely flexible when it comes to transferring property to children. This is because it enables parents to transfer their property to children using a variety of different techniques to provide for the management of that property until the child is old enough to manage it himself. In addition, wills also afford parents an invaluable opportunity to appoint personal guardians for their minor children.

The primary drawback of using a will, however, is that it can take several months (and sometimes years) to complete the probate process. This can prevent the transfer of assets to the beneficiaries named in the will for a prolonged period. Fortunately, there is several estate planning tools that can be utilized to avoid this situation, revocable living trusts being the most common.

Revocable Living Trusts

A revocable living trust is a type of 'inter vivos' (made between the living) trust used for estate planning purposes. Under a revocable living trust arrangement, a trust is created with the creator also acting as trustee of the trust. The creator then transfers legal ownership of some or all his personal property to the trust. However, as trustee of the trust, the creator maintains control over and use of the trust property after it has been received by the trust. He can therefore continue to enjoy it in almost the same way as he did when he held the property in his own name.

The trust agreement establishing the trust sets out (in much the same way as a will does) details of the persons who will be entitled to the trust assets following the creator's death. This entitlement may be to specific assets or to a share in the overall trust estate. The agreement also usually entitles the creator to add assets to or withdraw them from the trust property, change the terms of the trust, change the beneficiaries, make it irrevocable (incapable of change) and even revoke the trust at any time. If the trust is revoked, the creator will be entitled to the immediate return of the property held by the trust.

After the creator's death, the trust assets will pass to the beneficiaries named in the trust agreement. A person known as the successor trustee (which is a little like an executor) will be appointed under the trust agreement and will have the responsibility of transferring ownership of the assets in the trust to the beneficiaries named in the trust agreement. Once all the trust assets have been transferred to the named beneficiaries, the trust ceases to exist.

In most cases, the whole transfer process takes only a few weeks. However, if there is any tax payable, the process may be drawn out. Apart from the benefits associated with a speedy distribution of the trust assets, revocable living trusts are also beneficial from a cost perspective. In many cases, unless real estate needs to be transferred, there are rarely any lawyer or court fees to pay in connection with the winding up of the trust estate.

From an estate planning perspective, one of the most important features to note about a revocable living trust is that since the assets in the trust are legally owned by the trust, they will not form part of the creator's estate at the time of his death. As such, there will be no need for any of the assets held within the trust to go through the probate process. This is the reason why there can be a speedy distribution of those assets to the trust's beneficiaries and why probate fees are also reduced.

Revocable living trusts are quite easy to establish and, apart from avoiding probate, there are many other advantages to using living trusts as part of your overall estate plan. These reasons relate to the management of your assets during incapacity, privacy, and in some cases taxes.

Resource

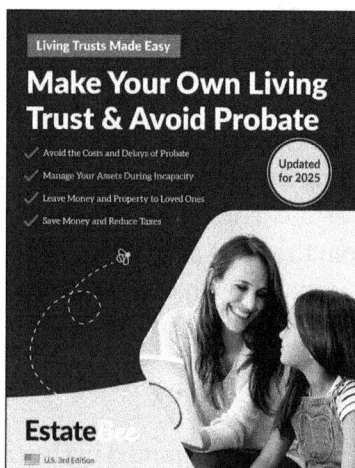

Make Your Own Living Trust & Avoid Probate

Living trusts are used to distribute a person's assets after they die in a manner that avoids the costs, delays, and publicity of probate. They also cater for the management of property during periods of incapacity.

This book will guide you step-by-step through the

process of creating your very own living trust, transferring assets to your living trust, and subsequently managing those assets. All relevant forms are included.

Get your copy at

www.estate-bee.com/product/make-your-own-living-trust-avoid-probate/

Joint Ownerships

Ordinarily, assets held in your sole name alone are subject to probate. By contrast, jointly held assets are not. Therefore, the need for probate can be reduced or eliminated by simply converting solely owned assets into jointly owned assets. This form of ownership is sometimes referred to as joint tenancy. With a joint tenancy, where one joint tenant dies, the surviving joint tenant inherits the deceased joint tenant's share of the jointly held property. More important, from a probate perspective, is the fact that jointly owned assets pass directly to the surviving joint tenant (who can be a friend or relative) on the death of the other joint tenant without the need for probate.

Pay-on-Death and Transfer-on-Death Accounts

Pay-on-death ("**POD**") accounts, otherwise known as Totten Trusts, represent one of the simplest means of keeping money out of probate and are offered by a variety of financial institutions including banks, savings and loan associations, and credit unions. A POD account is like a normal bank account save that it contains a designation identifying the person who will become entitled to the proceeds of that account on the death of the main account holder. When the account holder dies, the proceeds of the account automatically pass to the named beneficiary. The good thing is that this all happens outside of the probate process. The only documents that the beneficiary will need to collect the proceeds of the account will be the account holder's death certificate and some ID. Although, some institutions may require further documents to comply with internal regulations.

During the account holder's lifetime, the POD beneficiaries will have no rights whatsoever to access the proceeds of the account. In fact, the account holder remains free to (at any time) withdraw the monies in the account, remove the POD designation, change the POD designation, or even close the account. In some states, the POD designation is deemed to be revoked where the account holder gifts the proceeds of the account to a third party under the terms of his will.

The proceeds of the account will be deemed to be those of the account holder during his lifetime. As such, they can be reached by creditors who successfully sue the account holder for debts due or damages. However, once the account holder dies, the designated beneficiaries become entitled to the proceeds of the account. Where this happens, the account holder's creditors are generally unable to reach the funds. However, there are some exceptions to this general rule. As such, legal advice should be sought if a creditor seeks to recover the proceeds of the account from a designated beneficiary.

If the designated beneficiary predeceases the account holder, the gift to the beneficiary will usually fail and will not normally be saved by an anti-lapse statute. In which case, the proceeds of the account become part of the account holder's estate for probate purposes.

An account can be opened with a POD designation or such a designation can be added to an existing account by simply adding the name of the beneficiary to the account's mandate or signature card. For information on what exactly is required in each instance, you should contact your bank or a relevant financial institution.

Transfer-on-death ("TOD") accounts are like POD accounts but are more commonly used to transfer ownership of stocks, securities, bonds and units in mutual funds. If you wish to add a transfer-on-death designation to any of your securities, it is recommended that you speak to a broker.

Insurance Policies

If you have a life insurance policy but haven't designated a beneficiary, the monies payable upon your death will become part of your estate and will be distributed in accordance with the terms of your will or, if you have no will, in accordance with the rules of intestacy. As the insurance proceeds form part of your estate, any beneficiary entitled to them under your will or on intestacy will have to wait for the probate/administration of your estate to complete before being entitled to receive the proceeds. However, if you designate a specific beneficiary (and there can be more than one) under your policy, the proceeds will become payable to that beneficiary upon your death without the need to go through the probate process.

Probate Free Transfers of Assets

If you own boats or motor vehicles and their total value is less than a certain amount (usually between $25,000 and $75,000 depending on state law), then ownership of these vehicles can be transferred probate free to a surviving spouse or next-of-kin of the deceased.

In addition, any salary, wages, accumulated vacation time and sick benefits, plus any other fringe benefits, may be paid to a surviving spouse, registered partner, adult child, or next-of-kin of a deceased employee. That payment can usually take place probate free depending on the laws of the state in which the deceased was employed.

'Small Estates' Transfer Procedures

As mentioned already, depending on the value of your estate, it may be possible to avoid formal probate administration if that value is below a certain monetary amount. Where it is, your estate may be entitled to avail of a streamlined and simplified probate process for the transfer of small estates in lieu of a formal probate procedure. The definition of a small estate varies widely from state to state so you will need to check the laws in your state to determine the precise figure.

If your estate qualifies as a small estate, your executor or beneficiaries may be entitled to sign an *affidavit* to that effect and, on production of the affidavit and a copy of your death certificate, require the release of your property and money to him/them.

Planning for Incapacity – Power of Attorney for Finance & Property

A *power of attorney* is a legal document by which you can appoint and authorize another person (usually a trusted friend, family member, colleague or adviser) to act on your behalf in the event that you are unable to act yourself due to incapacity or otherwise.

There are two principal types of *powers of attorney*, an *ordinary power of attorney* and a *durable power of attorney*. Ordinary powers of attorney automatically come to an end if you become incapacitated. Durable powers of attorney, by contrast, do not come to an end if you become incapacitated and, in many cases, often only commence at such time. For this reason, durable powers of attorney are typically used for estate planning purposes.

Durable powers of attorney come in two forms – a durable general power of attorney and a durable limited power of attorney. Under a *durable general power of attorney*, your appointed agent will be authorized to act as your legal representative in relation to all your legal and financial affairs. In other words, your agent will **acting** in your name and on your behalf, be able to collect and disburse money; operate your bank accounts; buy and sell property; refurbish and rent out your property; and generally sign documents and deeds.

The authorization under a power of attorney will usually commence on the date specified in the document or, more commonly, on the date that you are determined to be incapacitated. The authorization will end when you revoke it (which, in the case of incapacity, you can only do if you regain capacity) or you die.

While the law varies from state to state, a person will usually be deemed to be 'incapable' or 'incapacitated' if they are either (i) unable to understand and process information that is relevant to making an informed decision and/or (ii) unable to evaluate the likely consequences of making that decision. In many cases, the procedure for determining whether a person is incapacitated is set out in the power of attorney document itself and typically involves assessments by medical physicians.

The second type of durable power of attorney is a *durable limited power of attorney*. This is like a durable general power of attorney except that it expressly limits the agent's authority to act on your behalf. In this regard, you can set out exactly what the agent can to and what he cannot. For example, you might authorize him to deal with a particular business you own and nothing else. The choice is yours.

Resource

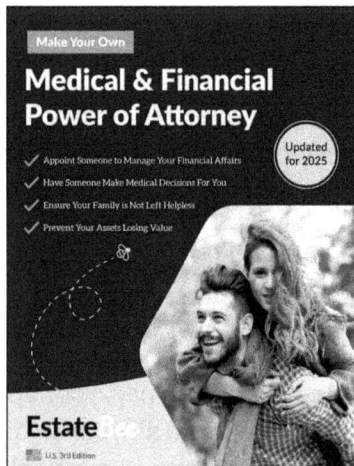

Make Your Own Medical & Financial Powers of Attorney

The importance of having powers of attorney is often underappreciated. They allow people you trust to manage your property and financial affairs during periods in which you are incapacitated; as well as make medical decisions on your behalf based on the instructions in your power of attorney document. This ensures that your affairs don't go unmanaged if you are incapacitated and you don't receive any unwanted medical treatments.

This book provides all the necessary documents and step-by-step instructions to make a power of attorney to cover virtually any situation.

Get your copy at

www.estate-bee.com/product/make-your-own-medical-financial-powers-of-attorney

If you fail to make a power of attorney, your family may have to formally apply to court to have a guardian or conservator appointed to manage your legal and financial affairs. This person, who may or may not be a family member, will have power to make decisions on your behalf and generally to manage your affairs as he sees fit – without regard to your wishes or those of your family. Of course, the situation can be avoided by having a power of attorney.

In broad terms, the general view is that, (i) the more complex and sensitive your affairs are, (ii) the higher the standard of living your family is accustomed to, and/or (iii) the more disruptive any disability to perform on your part would be — the greater the need to make a power of attorney to protect your assets and provide for your family.

Planning for Incapacity – Advance Healthcare Directives

Advance healthcare directives enable you to instruct others about the medical care you would like to receive if you are unable to make decisions for yourself or communicate those decisions. There are two specific types of healthcare directives to consider, each with differing features. These are living wills and healthcare powers of attorney.

Living Wills

A living will is a legal document that allows you to instruct healthcare providers in relation to the use or non-use of certain life-sustaining medical treatments in the event that you are terminally ill or permanently unconscious and unable to communicate your own wishes.

To understand the uses of a living will, it is useful to define some medical terms:

- Life-sustaining medical treatment means any form of healthcare that will serve mainly to prolong or delay the process of dying.
- Terminal illness or terminal condition means an irreversible, incurable, and untreatable condition caused by disease, illness or injury.
- Permanently unconscious means an irreversible condition in which you are permanently unaware of yourself and your surroundings.
- Comfort care or palliative care means any measure taken to diminish pain or discomfort, but not to postpone death.

You can use a living will to set out your preferences in relation to the receipt or non-receipt of nutrition, hydration, blood, CPR, mechanical respiration, and much more. However, even where you have a living will, healthcare personnel will still provide comfort care to you. They generally will not stand by and leave you in severe physical pain, for example.

The way a living will works is quite straightforward. In most states, two doctors must agree that the use of medical procedures will only prolong the dying process and that, absent the use of such procedures, death would occur in the short term. If both doctors agree that this is the case, then the medical procedures may be withdrawn or withheld, depending on the contents of the living will.

Resource

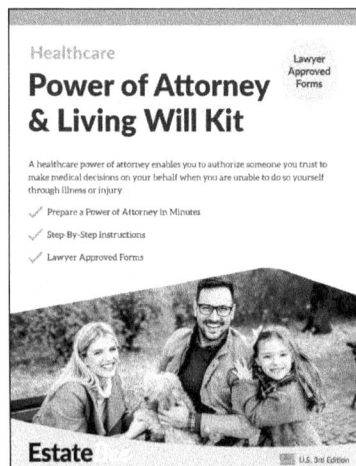

Healthcare
Power of Attorney & Living Will Kit

Lawyer Approved Forms

A healthcare power of attorney enables you to authorize someone you trust to make medical decisions on your behalf when you are unable to do so yourself through illness or injury.

✓ Prepare a Power of Attorney in Minutes

✓ Step-By-Step Instructions

✓ Lawyer Approved Forms

Estate

U.S. 3rd Edition

Healthcare Power of Attorney & Living Will Kit

Do you want a say in what life sustaining medical treatments you receive during periods in which you are incapacitated and either in a permanent state of unconsciousness or suffering from a terminal illness? Well if so, you must have a living will!

This book will introduce you to living wills, the types of medical procedures that they cover, the matters that you need to consider when making them and, of course, provide you with all the relevant forms you need to make your own living will.

Get your copy at

www.estate-bee.com/product/helathcare-power-of-attorney-living-will-kit/

Other names for living wills include 'instructions', 'directive to physicians' and 'declaration'.

Healthcare Power of Attorney

Two of the principal limitations of living wills is that they only (i) become effective when you are terminally ill, or permanently unconscious, and unable to communicate your wishes and (ii) deal with the receipt of life sustaining treatments – as opposed to any other kind of treatments.

On the other hand, a healthcare power of attorney allows you to appoint someone (an agent) to make all kinds of medical decisions for you irrespective of whether you are terminally ill or permanently unconscious. The agent's authority will usually only become effective once your attending physician determines that you have lost the capacity to make informed healthcare decisions. For so long as you have the capacity to make your own decisions, you retain the right to make all your own medical and healthcare decisions.

The authority of your agent to make healthcare decisions for you generally includes the authority to give informed consent; refuse to give informed consent; or withdraw informed consent for any care, treatment, service, or procedure designed to maintain, diagnose, or treat a physical or mental condition. However, you can expressly limit your agent's authority under a power of attorney if you wish.

Guardians

If you are a parent, you will need to make proper arrangements for the future care of your children in case you and the children's other parent die before they grow up. This can be achieved by appointing a guardian who will be responsible for the care, welfare, and education of your children. That appointment can be made in a will or in a formal guardianship agreement.

Funeral Arrangements

Every good estate plan should include a funeral plan but, despite the advantages, almost 70% of people die without a pre-arranged plan. A funeral plan provides certainty by enabling you to clearly instruct your family in relation to sensitive matters such as whether you would prefer burial or cremation, where you want to be interred, the type of funeral service you would like, and much more. Without such a plan, your family will make the choices for you.

Resource

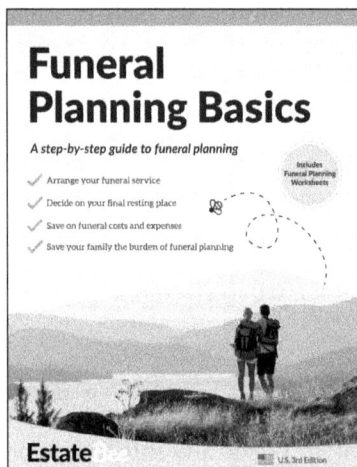

"Funeral Planning Basics - A Step-By-Step Guide to Funeral Planning"

Through proper funeral planning, you can ensure that your loved ones are not confronted with the unnecessary burden of having to plan a funeral at a time that is already very traumatic for them.

This book will introduce you to issues such as organ donations, purchasing caskets, cremation, burial, purchasing grave plots, organization of funeral services, legal and financial issues, costs of prearranging a funeral, how to save money on funerals, how to finance funerals and much more.

Get your copy at:

www.estate-bee.com/product/funeral-planning-basics/

CHAPTER 8

Estate Taxes

Introduction

The information in this section is provided as a brief overview of taxation in the United States. If you have any tax queries relating to the disposal or distribution of your estate, it is recommend that you speak to a qualified lawyer or tax advisor.

Estate Taxes

When accountants, lawyers and others who deal with these matters refer to 'estate tax' they are usually referring to federal tax, not state tax. This distinction is made for three main reasons: (i) many states do not impose an inheritance or death tax; (ii) federal tax is likely to devour more of an estate than state tax will; and (iii) reducing the federal estate tax will often result in a reduction of state taxes as well.

Federal Estate and Gift Tax

The U.S. tax system generally taxes transfers of wealth. This means the federal government usually charges a tax when money or other assets are transferred from one person to another. Keeping this general rule in mind helps to understand estate and gift taxes.

Gift tax, unlike most income taxes, is assessed on the giver, and not the receiver. As such, if you make a gift of cash or an asset to someone, you will be assessed to a gift tax unless you fall within the scope of the exceptions set out under the headings below. When gift tax is payable, you will need to record details of the gift on IRS form 709. Like many other tax forms, the gift tax form is generally due April 15th in the year following the year in which you made the gift.

Similarly, when you die, another transfer of assets takes place from you to someone else. Like the gift tax, the estate tax is imposed on the giver, which in that case will be your estate. A federal estate tax return is reported on IRS form 706 and is due to be filed with the IRS within nine months of the date of your death unless extended.

Everyone's "Coupon"

The gift and estate tax have to be considered together, because they are intertwined in that both are taken into account when calculating the maximum amount that you can give away or, if you die, your estate can transfer without incurring a charge to tax. Simply speaking, the maximum amount you can transfer without incurring gift or estate tax is like a "coupon". When the value of your gifts and estate are calculated, you can apply this "coupon" to minimize or avoid the tax. You will only have to pay gift or estate tax if your gifts and/or transfers exceed this "coupon" amount.

For example, in 2025 the "coupon" for **gifts** is $13,990,000 . That means that you can transfer up to $13,990,000 in gifts during your lifetime and there won't be any gift tax due. That means that most Americans will not end up paying estate tax.

If a gift is made to someone other than your spouse, it won't matter who received the gift just that the total value of gifts didn't exceed the "coupon". However, if you exceed the value of the "coupon", you'll owe tax on the excess gift(s). Under current law, the rate of gift tax varies based on the year of the gift. A chart detailing the rate of gift and estate tax can be found under the heading "How to Determine the Estate Tax".

For example, if you give $5,000,000 of taxable gifts to each of your three children over your lifetime, you'll have made $15,000,000 in taxable gifts. You can use your "coupon" to avoid tax on the first $13,990,000 but you'll owe tax on the other $1,010,000 .

How does this relate to estate taxes? Well, for most years, you also have a "coupon" for estate taxes. However, as the government views every dollar you gave away during your lifetime as a dollar less that can be taxed in your estate when you die, this "coupon" will be reduced by the amount of the gift tax "coupon" that you have used during your lifetime. So, while there is also a "coupon" for estate tax, it is linked to the gift tax "coupon"; and more specifically to the amount of that gift tax "coupon" that you have already used.

Example: Let's say you made those three $15,000,000 gifts to your children, and still had $5 million in your taxable estate when you died in 2025. In 2025, the estate tax "coupon" is $13,990,000 , so at first blush we might calculate that your estate owes estate tax on $1,010,000 , which is the difference between the $15 million value of your estate and the estate tax "coupon".

However, that calculation would be wrong because the estate tax "coupon" is reduced by any gift tax "coupon" that you have already used. So, because you used the full $13,990,000 gift tax "coupon" during your lifetime, your estate tax "coupon" is reduced by $13,990,000 to $0. On the other hand, if you had used only $1,000,000 of your gift tax "coupon", your estate tax "coupon" would be $12,990,000 ($13,990,000 estate tax "coupon" less $1,000,000 of gift tax "coupon" used).

Example of Coupon

Anna gave James and John a total of $10 million during her lifetime that used up most of her lifetime gifting exemption of $13,990,000 . Anna died in 2025. The estate tax threshold in 2025 was $13,990,000. However, to determine whether Anna had reached her estate tax exemption threshold, the gifts she made during her lifetime will be taken into account. As such, on her death, her exemption would only be $3,990,000 ($13,990,000 million less the $10,000,000 gift tax exemption used).

How to Determine the Estate Tax?

The first question to ask when trying to determine the amount of federal estate tax which might be due by your estate is "What is the fair market value of everything you own, control, or have an interest in at the date of your death?" In answering this question, you will need to include all assets you own such as cash, investments, real estate, and personal property such as cars, boats, art and the like. Estate tax is also levied on the life insurance policies in your name where you have a right of ownership in the policy.

The total value of all of these items is called your "gross estate". Your taxable estate is your gross estate less certain deductions. These deductions may include mortgages on your assets, debts you owe, estate administration expenses, property that passes automatically to your surviving spouse on your death, and bequests to qualified charities (more on the deductions for spouses and charities below). The value of your gross estate minus these deductions is referred to as your "taxable estate".

Once you have calculated your taxable estate, estate tax may be owed if the value of the taxable estate exceeds the unused portion of your estate tax "coupon."

Just as the value of the "coupon" changes depending on the year in which you make a gift or die, the percentage of the tax assessment also changes.

Year of Gift/Death	Maximum Gift Tax	Maximum Estate Tax
2009	45%	45%
2010	35%	N/A
2011 & 2012	35%	35%
2013 - 2025 and beyond	40%	40%

State Taxes

Not every state imposes a separate state tax on estates or inheritances. Florida, for instance, imposes no state death tax. Where there is such a tax, it is likely to be one (or a combination) of three types of tax: (1) death tax, (2) inheritance tax, or (3) pick-up tax.

State Death Taxes

Generally, when people use the phrase "death tax", they are referring to state taxes levied on a deceased person's estate on their death. The amount of state tax due, if any, is determined on a state-by-state basis according to that state's tax laws and is often calculated in a manner similar to federal estate tax.

State Inheritance Taxes

In states with inheritance tax laws, inheritance tax is usually paid by the person who receives assets either under a will or on intestacy. In some states, the tax is levied on the estate itself so that the tax must be paid by the estate before calculating what can be distributed to beneficiaries. One tax rate may apply to all assets in the estate, or the rate may vary depending upon who receives what property. Generally, the closer the person receiving a gift from the deceased is to the deceased (in terms of blood line), the lower the tax rate on the transfer of property to that person. Thus, depending on what class the beneficiary falls into, he or she will be taxed at a specific rate.

States with Inheritance Taxes or State Estate Taxes			
State	Tax Collected	State	Tax Collected
Connecticut	Estate Tax	Minnesota	Estate Tax
Delaware	Estate Tax, expired July 1, 2013	Nebraska	Inheritance Tax
District of Colombia	Estate Tax	New Jersey	Estate Tax and Inheritance Tax
Hawaii	Estate Tax	New York	Estate Tax
Illinois	Estate Tax	Oregon	Estate Tax
Iowa	Inheritance Tax	Pennsylvania	Inheritance Tax
Kentucky	Inheritance Tax	Rhode Island	Estate Tax
Maine	Estate Tax	Tennessee	Estate Tax
Maryland	Estate Tax & Inheritance Tax	Vermont	Estate Tax
Massachusetts	Estate Tax	Washington	Estate Tax

State "Pick-Up" Taxes

Some states base all or a portion of their state death tax on the amount of credit that the federal estate tax used to allow for state death taxes. Prior to 2005, federal estate taxes could be reduced by a credit for the amount of state death taxes paid. The result was that the federal estate tax was a "maximum" tax that was paid partly to the state and partly to the federal government. Many states therefore would "pick-up" their tax revenue by pegging their state death taxes at the amount of the federal credit that you could claim for state death taxes. After 2001, the federal government gradually eliminated the credit for state death taxes. However, some states chose to continue to charge a pick-up tax based on what the federal credit was in 2001, even though the federal credit is no longer available.

For all three of the types of tax a state might assess, some states will have a "coupon" equal to the federal tax "coupon", meaning that if there is no federal estate tax there is no state estate tax. However, many states have chosen not to increase their "coupons" at the same rate that the federal law does, so the state "coupon" may be smaller, resulting in state estate tax being payable even where federal estate tax is not payable.

At the time of writing, 12 states and the District of Columbia still collect pick up taxes: Connecticut, Hawaii, Illinoi, Minnesota, Oregon, Maine, Maryland, Massachusetts, New York, Rhode Island, Vermont, and Washington.

Marital Deduction

Remember the gift and estate tax "coupon" for federal taxes? Historically, it was unique to each individual/estate and could not be used by anyone else. That meant that you had a "coupon" and your spouse had a "coupon" and they were non-transferable.

The "coupons" are not used up by gifts made or estates transferred to a spouse who is a U.S. citizen. Instead, federal gift/estate tax applies an unlimited deduction to those transfers. In other words, you can gift or transfer an unlimited amount of property to your U.S. citizen spouse and there is no gift or estate tax on that transfer.

That's the good news. The bad news is that the marital deduction is, in some ways, just a waiting game whereby the government allows you to transfer your property tax free to your spouse with the view that it will later be taxed when your spouse dies or gives it away. As your spouse could not use your gift/estate tax "coupon" prior to the introduction of the Tax Relief, Unemployment Insurance Reauthorization, and Job Creation Act of 2010, in December 2010, that meant that your spouse had more to transfer to her beneficiaries and heirs but without the benefit of an increased the "coupon". However, in December 2010, President Obama signed this legislation into law which entitled a person to use any unused element of his or her deceased spouse's coupon. However, that right could be lost if the surviving spouse remarried and his/her new spouse predeceased him/her.

Consider this example: Your last will & testament provides for your spouse to inherit everything you own when you die. At your death, your net taxable estate is $15,000,000 and your spouse also has an estate worth $15,000,000. Since your spouse was the recipient of your estate, the unlimited marital deduction applies and there is no estate tax due as a result of your death regardless of the applicable "coupon". If your spouse dies in 2025, under current law your spouse's maximum "coupon" will be $27,980,000 - $13,990,000 of his or her own plus $13,990,000 of yours – assuming neither of you previously used any element of your coupon. Of course, to the extent that either of you used your coupon, this amount will be deducted from the $27,980,000 coupon. Ultimately, your spouse's estate will be subject to tax on the excess of "$2,020,000 ($30,000,0000 - $27,980,000) At a tax rate of 40%, that translates to a tax of "$808,000.

Of course, these thresholds are so high most people won't have to concern themselves too much about them.

Important Note

A surviving spouse will lose the right to use his or her deceased spouse's coupon if he or she remarries!

Non-Citizen Spouses

The unlimited marital deduction is available only when you give or leave your assets to a spouse who is a U.S. citizen at the time the transfer is made. Some types of credit shelter trust planning mechanisms are also only effective if your spouse is a U.S. citizen. If your spouse is not a citizen, your estate plan must include more sophisticated trust planning designed to keep the assets in the United States managed by a U.S. trustee so that the trust can qualify for the marital deduction that is otherwise available to U.S. citizen spouses. This is called a Qualified Domestic Trust, or QDOT. For more information, speak to an attorney.

Charitable Deductions

You probably already know that you get an income tax deduction when you donate to a charity during your lifetime. You can also save on estate taxes by giving to charity. Any bequest you make from your estate to a qualified charity is exempt from federal estate tax. You can also combine estate tax planning and income tax planning by setting up a trust with a charity as one of the beneficiaries.

Charitable Remainder Trust

The most common charitable trust is a charitable remainder trust, or CRT. With this type of trust, you donate an asset or assets to the trust during your lifetime. You can continue to get some income from the trust assets, but the charity gets the remainder of what is in the trust when you die or when the term of the trust otherwise ends. Because you have donated to the trust, you will be allowed to take an income tax deduction equal to the estimated value of the charity's remainder. You have also removed the asset in the trust from your estate, so it will not be subject to estate taxes when you die. Yet you still can enjoy a regular payout from the trust assets. The amount of income you get from the trust may be either a fixed percentage of the assets you donated to the trust or a percentage of the trust's value each year. Of course, if you choose to peg your payment on the value of the trust, your payment will fluctuate as the value of the assets in the trust fluctuates.

Some CRTs are especially attractive if you have assets that have appreciated in value. By placing the asset into the trust, you may be able to minimize the capital gains taxes you would otherwise have had to pay when you sold the asset.

Let us look at how a CRT would work in an example: Anna and David own vacant land that they purchased many years ago. The value of the land has gone up considerably, so they would have to pay significant capital gains tax if they sold it. Yet, the land is not producing any income for them in their retirement. Rather than sell the land, pay the capital gains tax, and then invest the after-tax proceeds to produce income, they decide to create a CRT and donate the land to the trust. Once the land has been transferred to the trust, the trust is free to sell the land without having to pay any capital gains tax on the sale. The CRT can then use the proceeds of sale to provide an income to Anna and David for as long as any one of them is alive. After they both die, the remainder of the trust assets can be given to a charity of their choosing.

Having established the CRT and transferred the land to it, Anna and David take an immediate income tax deduction for the estimated value of the amount that the trust will give to their chosen charity. In addition, they will receive income annually from the trust. They may have to pay some tax on the income they receive from the trust, but often it is not as much as they would have had to pay upfront if they had just sold the land. Furthermore, the value of the land is no longer in their estates, so there will not be any estate tax assessed on that value – which is a further cost saving to their estate.

Charitable Lead Trust

Another type of charitable trust is a charitable lead trust ("CLT"). With a CLT, you transfer property to a trust that then pays an annual income ("the lead") to a charity. When the trust terminates after a specified number of years, the remaining assets left in the trust go to a person or persons you name, such as your children. Generally, you will not get an income tax deduction for giving any property to a CLT, but you won't pay any gift tax and you have removed some of the value of the asset from your estate. A CLT can be a good choice for an asset that is expected to appreciate in the future, so that the appreciated value will not be in your estate.

Another example: Assume that Anna and David in the example above have land that they expect to be worth much more in the coming years as the area around the land is developed. They decide to establish a charitable lead trust that in five years will begin to pay a percentage of the trust assets to their favorite charity. When the trust is terminated in fifteen years, the assets remaining in the trust will go to their grandchildren. There may be a taxable gift to the grandchildren depending on the estimated value of the gift that passes to them, but that estimated value will be based on the value of the land now, and will not include the high appreciation expected in the near future. Anna and David have removed the value of the asset from their estate, provided for their favorite charity, and assured that the land as it appreciates will benefit their grandchildren in the future.

For more information on CLTs, speak to your attorney or tax advisor.

Other Ways to Reduce Estate Taxes

Federal estate tax can be reduced through a variety of other legitimate estate planning techniques. Since the "coupon" has increased to $13,990,000 per person, those with large estates over this amount could benefit from considering some of the methods listed below to reduce potential estate tax liability. The advantages and disadvantages of these techniques vary greatly depending on the individual circumstances of the persons using them. That is why having an experienced attorney or tax advisor can be beneficial as you consider how these techniques fit your situation.

Lifetime Gifts

A gift made to a spouse who is a U.S. citizen is not taxed, regardless of the value of the gift. Gifts made to noncitizen spouses are tax free up to $190,000 for 2025.

Under federal tax law, some gifts incur no gift tax, don't require filing of a gift tax return, and don't even use up any of your "coupon". This amount is pegged to inflation so it will vary each year. For example, in 2025, you may make an annual tax-exempt gift to any one person provided the total amount of gifts to that person during the calendar year does not exceed $19,000. This exemption applies to each person making a gift which means that if both you and your spouse utilize this estate planning tool, you could collectively reduce your estate by giving away $36,000 a year to any number of beneficiaries, free of any federal gift tax. The annual exemption amount changes based on inflation, but over a period of several years the amount of money that you and your spouse (or partner) could transfer to your intended beneficiaries under this method could be quite substantial.

You can also make tax-free gifts by paying someone's medical expenses or tuition bills provided that you pay the bill directly to the medical or educational institution. Gifts of this type are not subject to the annual exemption limits and could be in any amount.

Making lifetime gifts as described above removes the gifted assets from your estate, potentially reducing the amount your estate would otherwise have to pay in federal estate tax. However, during most years, lifetime gifts may be less advantageous than inheritances when we consider the effect of capital gains taxes. Capital gain is the amount you get when you sell the asset minus your basis. Broadly speaking, basis is the amount you have invested in the asset. So, if you sell an asset for $100 where your basis was $10, you will have a capital gain of $90 that is subject to capital gains tax. When you make a gift during your lifetime, the recipient of the gift has the same basis in the gifted asset as you have. As a result, the $100 asset will have the same $90 capital gain when the recipient sells it as you would have incurred if you had sold it. The transfer of the initial $10 basis to the recipient in this manner is referred to as a "carry-over basis".

However, in most years if you leave the asset as an inheritance rather than a lifetime gift, your recipient now gets a "stepped up basis" to the value of the asset on the date that you died. In the case of our $100 asset, if the value was $100 when you died, the recipient would now have a basis of $100 (rather than a carry-over basis of $10). If the recipient sells the asset for $100, there will be no capital gains subject to tax. Since capital gains taxes are currently around 15%, gifting the asset would have cost the recipient $13.50 in capital gains tax ($90 x .15) while inheriting the asset wouldn't have incurred any tax. This difference in basis is why it is important to consult a tax advisor before making significant lifetime gifts as part of your estate planning.

Irrevocable Life Insurance Trusts

An irrevocable life insurance trust creates a trust that is used exclusively to own life insurance. The trust purchases life insurance on your life, and you make gifts to the trust to pay the premiums. The trust may not be revoked and once you place funds into the trust, they cannot be taken back. Upon your death, the life insurance payout to your trust is distributed according to the terms of the trust. Because you do not control the life insurance, it is not considered part of your taxable estate and thus no federal estate taxes are due when the payout is made.

Family Limited Partnerships

A family limited partnership helps families transfer ownership of their closely held businesses to the next generation of business managers. A family limited partnership, or FLP, is created to hold and manage assets. You may transfer those assets to the FLP in exchange for your interest in the partnership. You then gift some of your partnership interest to your children, perhaps over several years.

FLPs can save estate taxes in two ways. First, they can remove from your estate now assets that are likely to appreciate in value. Even though the asset is removed from the estate, you may retain control over the partnership and therefore have continued control over how the asset is managed. Second, the percentage gift you make to your children in an FLP may be valued at less than the same percentage of the value of the underlying assets in the partnership.

For example, assume you establish a partnership with three pieces of real estate each valued at $500,000. The value of the assets in the partnership total $1,500,000. Then you gift a ten percent interest in the partnership to your son. While ten percent of the value of the partnership assets is $150,000 ($1,500,000 x .10), the value of a ten percent interest in the partnership may be appreciably less than $150,000. This is because as a ten percent owner your son does not have control over the assets and there isn't likely to be someone willing to pay him $150,000 for the chance to be a minority partner that lacks control. This has the effect of reducing the fair market value of the 10% interest below that of an equivalent percentage value of the underlying properties. In fact, the real value of the ten percent partnership interest depends on many factors, which is why you must be prepared to get a qualified appraisal on the gift when you use an FLP in your planning. For more information, speak to your attorney or tax advisor.

Special Use Real Estate Valuation

Generally, real estate you transfer by way of a gift or on your death is valued based on the assumption that the real estate will be sold for its "highest and best use" value. For example, farmland may be worth much more if it was sold for residential development than as agricultural land. However, you or your estate may be able to claim that the real estate should be valued based on its "actual use" value rather than the "highest and best use" value. This can result in significant tax savings, especially if your family intends to continue using the land as farmland rather than selling it to a developer. Special use valuation is complicated and generally requires the assistance of an experienced attorney and valuation agent.

Conclusion

Estate taxes and estate tax planning are a complicated area of the law. If you have an estate greater than a million dollars or have other special circumstances, we recommend that you seek professional advice before employing any of the tax reduction strategies referred to in this chapter.

CHAPTER 9

Getting Organized and Making Your Will

Before we turn to formalities and forms, let's recap why and how you should make an effective will to protect your family members and your estate.

Before You Start

Many people believe that the quality of preparation determines the quality of the job. The best preparation for making a will begins with some expert advice. Consult a tax specialist or estate-planning attorney and discuss your situation. Find out if you need more than a simple will. Is there an advantage to setting up a living trust? How about a living will or a healthcare power of attorney?

Consider the wisdom of writing your own will versus hiring a professional. Think carefully: is a disgruntled family member likely to contest the will? If so, are they more likely to attack your will if it is vulnerable to challenges? Remember, this person will almost certainly consult an attorney before deciding what to do. Ask your attorney what their advice would be if you came to them with a similar situation. Naturally, they would want to see the will you were challenging first. Would they prefer to be contesting a self-made will, or a professionally drafted one? Or do they not have a preference?

Review Online Will Resources

If you are considering making your own will, look at some of the online offerings. Find out whether they live up to their promise to cover all the areas you need to know about to make an effective will. Additionally, ascertain whether the package covers any extra provisions that you may need to create. You may need to create living trusts, living wills, and financial and healthcare powers of attorney in addition to your will. Check and see if the product offers state-specific wills rather than a generic, "one-size-fits-all" format.

Of course, feel free to use the sample forms provided at the back of this book and to explore any of the other titles in EstateBee's estate planning range.

Get Organized

Start by making some lists. Use the forms contained in the back of the book or simply download them from www.Estate-Bee.com.

- List your objectives in distributing your estate.
- List your assets, including loans owed to you.
- List what you owe to others, including mortgages, car loans, credit cards, and any other debts owed.
- List the family members whom you wish to benefit under your will.
- List any friends and others you would like to benefit (e.g. your faithful housekeeper of many years, or the friend who has stood by you through all your highs and lows).
- Note your relationship to each beneficiary.
- List any charitable gifts you wish to make.
- List the items, or cash amounts, that you want each beneficiary to receive.
- When you have allocated specific bequests and cash legacies, consider the balance of your estate. Is there enough to pay debts and taxes?
- Determine whether the remaining balance is best handled by bundling it into one category, under the heading of the 'remainder' or the 'residue' of your estate, and then leaving it in equal (or non-equal) shares to a named group or class of beneficiaries.

Important Tip

Do not forget to include a residuary clause in your will. Even if you think that you have already gifted all your property under your will, you should still include this clause. Not only does it cover the situation where you may have accidentally forgotten to gift an asset, but it could also avoid intestate administration in relation to any non-disposed assets.

Appoint One or More Executors

One of the most important steps in ensuring the good administration of the estate is to choose a good and capable executor (or executors). Two is a recommended number of executors unless your estate is large and complex and needs to have 'board meetings' of experienced people to manage your affairs through to the wind-up stage.

A son, daughter or other close family member is usually the best place to start. A close and trusted friend would also be a great executor. The second executor/executrix might be another son or daughter, your sibling, or your lawyer or accountant. Again, before appointing an executor, be sure to ask whether they would be willing and able to act.

Another option is to retain a professional trust company to act as executor, trustee, or both. There will be fees to pay and they will vary according to the size of the estate, but you can generally count on trust companies to act and to invest very conservatively in their administration of the estate. Trust companies do present a definite alternative if you lack confidence in your other options or find it difficult to choose between them.

Appoint a Testamentary Guardian for Your Minor Children

If you have minor children, then the first question will be whether their other parent or your spouse is still there to care for them. Your will should include a provision that states 'If my spouse Alex Doe should predecease me, then I appoint Richard Roe as testamentary guardian of my minor children'. Keep in mind that any guardian must be an adult. In practice, it is common to appoint one's brother or sister and sometimes their spouse to take on this role, provided they are willing and able to do so.

In the case of a young family, grandparents might be logical testamentary guardians. If your parents or parents-in-law should predecease you, you would simply substitute another party or parties.

Distribution of Property Overseas

As more people invest in foreign property it has become increasingly important to take account of foreign assets in the preparation of your will or estate plan. More importantly, however, is the necessity to ensure that you do not inadvertently revoke an existing will. Generally, foreign property is subject to the succession laws of the country in which the property is situated. As such, it becomes necessary to execute a will dealing with your property in that country to record your wishes in relation to foreign property. To prevent any new 'local' will from revoking a will covering property located in a foreign jurisdiction, it is necessary to insert a clause in your local will stating that it does not relate to any property held outside this jurisdiction. A similar clause should be inserted into any foreign wills so that they do not revoke any wills made by you in the United States. In other words, it is recommended that you prepare separate will documents in each country where your assets are located.

As there are various estate taxation systems in existence in other countries, it is highly advisable to seek the advice of a national lawyer in the country in which your foreign assets are held.

Execute Your Will in the Prescribed Fashion

State laws set out the formal requirements for executing a will. While these laws are similar in each state, you should still check the specific requirements in your state. In general, however, a 'best practice' guide for executing your will could be summarized as follows:

- Write your initials, in the presence of two witnesses (three in Vermont), at the bottom of each page of your will, except the last (signature) page.

- each of the witnesses should, in your presence and in the presence of each other, initial each page next to where you just placed your initials.

- insert the date on which you are signing the will in the space provided on the final page of the will.

- write your initials beside where you inserted the date.

- each of the witnesses should, in your presence and in the presence of each other, write their initials beside where you placed your initials (i.e. beside the date).

- you must sign your ordinary signature, using a pen, in the space provided on the final page.

- each witness must, in your presence and in the presence of each other, write his name and address in the space provided on the final page of the will and then sign his name with his normal signature.

While the actual execution of your will should be relatively straightforward, there are several additional rules that apply when executing the will. These rules relate specifically to witnesses and notarization.

Witnesses should be at least 18 years of age and should not be a spouse or a beneficiary under the will (or a spouse of such beneficiary), as this could nullify any gifts made to them under the will.

Finally, once the will is executed, remember to keep it in a safe place. You should also consider informing the executor or even a close family member or friend of the location of the will so that it can be located when needed.

Important Tip

Generally, a will must be signed by you or by someone directed to do so on your behalf. Signatures may include marks, initials, a rubber stamp, a 'nickname' or even a former name.

Consider Related Documentation

Consider whether you need a living will, a living trust, and/or a power of attorney to round out your appropriate documentation. For a discussion of the nature and applicability of these documents, please see our books on each of these topics.

Cash Reserves During Administration

Ensure that your family has an available reserve of cash to use until your estate has been properly administered. Draft the will and prepare your estate plan so that sufficient funds will be available to facilitate the payment of funeral and testamentary expenses and your family's living expenses.

Alternatively, a small life insurance policy can be taken out on your life with your spouse as a beneficiary. If you keep this policy to a modest level (say $50,000 or $100,000) it generally results in a quicker payout on that policy, and avoids the 'moral risk' assessment delays that may accompany a claim for half a million or a million dollars.

Location of Your Will

Once your will is written, place it in a safe place that is accessible to your executors after your death. You can of course keep it in a safe deposit box but be aware that in some states your safe deposit box is sealed upon your death, so this may not always be the safest place to keep a will. Make sure that a close friend, relative or your executor knows where to find the will. If you had an attorney prepare your will, it would be useful to have him retain the original in his strong room or safe, or even retain a copy with a note stating where the original can be found.

CHAPTER 10

Reviewing and Updating Your Will

Reviewing Your Will

Your task as executor is not completed by simply making your will. In fact, it is recommended that you review and update your important legal documents on a regular basis to ensure that they reflect your current wishes and intentions. This includes any wills, powers of attorney, and estate plans you may have.

You should review your will and your estate plan periodically. Changes in tax law, property holding, family (marriage, death, divorce) and simple inflation in values can affect the intended results outlined by your will. Review your will annually if possible; and at least every two to three years (if not annually). These types of reviews have the added advantage of keeping you reasonably current with major changes in your financial circumstances.

For instance,

- Perhaps you remarried in the last twelve months, and 'inherited' a new stepchild or two, yet neither your new spouse nor your stepchildren are mentioned in your will.

- Maybe you left various blocks of shares to different children. One block has more than doubled in value, while another is practically worthless with the primary company in the portfolio going into liquidation. Yet you meant your children to share equally.

- Perhaps a small parcel of land you left to your cousin has suddenly quadrupled in price, due to a big new resort and shopping-town project getting the go–ahead. The value of their inheritance may be far more than you intended to leave them.

Consider your position carefully, and act prudently making changes which ought to be made in the circumstances.

Changing Your Will

As you will have just seen, there will always be important changes in your life that affect how you would like to distribute your estate following your death. These changes may be minor or peripheral, not requiring any great adjustment in your intentions or plans. On the other hand, they may be substantial such as in the case of births, deaths, divorce, remarriage, asset growth or diminution, new probate laws and taxes, or a move to or from a community property state.

These substantial changes, as well as changes in relationships and circumstances, often require changes to your will. When this happens, there are two options: make a new will in light of the new circumstances or amend the present will. Of course, there is a third option. You can do nothing and let the cards fall where they may.

If you perceive any required change/changes as sweeping and fundamental, it is probably time for a new will. On the other hand, if only one person or clause is affected, or the change is relatively minor, there is no reason why the alteration could not be made using a codicil.

Using a Codicil

There are specific legal procedures for making changes to a will. To make a valid change to a will, you must either make a new will or add a "codicil," which is an amendment to the will. A codicil is simply a testamentary document that amends rather than replaces an existing will. It requires the same formalities as to execution as a will. You can use different witnesses, but it is sometimes better (if they can be easily found) to use the same people who witnessed the original will.

Again, it's desirable that a witness to a codicil is not a beneficiary, as this precludes them from inheriting in some states.

Sometimes probate courts are faced with interpreting whether a testamentary document executed after the date of a will is intended as a new will, or merely as a codicil. If the document does not entirely revoke the earlier will, and doesn't completely dispose of the testator's estate, the presumption is that the document is a codicil. The prudent option is to avoid this difficulty by clearly labeling the new document 'codicil'.

If there is room, a codicil is normally added to the original will, immediately beneath the signatures. Note that it must be typed, not handwritten, to avoid being struck down in certain states. If there is no room to add a codicil after the signatures, it should be typed on a separate sheet of paper and attached to the original will. In fact, it is often best to start on a separate sheet of paper – and we recommend this approach.

Resource

How to make a.....

Codicil to a Last Will & Testament Kit

Lawyer Approved Forms

Have your personal circumstances changed? Do you need to update your Last Will & Testament? This legal kit allows you to amend your Will without needing a lawyer.

✓ Prepare a Codicil in Minutes
✓ Step-By-Step Instructions
✓ Lawyer Approved Forms

Estate
U.S. 3rd Edition

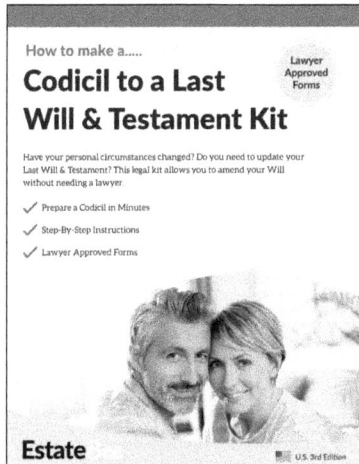

Full details on how to prepare a codicil are contained in our kit entitled "**How to Make a Codicil to Your Last Will & Testament**".

Get your copy at:

www.estate-bee.com/product/codicil-to-last-will-testament-kit/

Revoking Your Will

If you need to revoke your will outright, you may do so in several ways:

• draft a new will or codicil.

- physically destroy the old will.

- a will can be revoked by marriage unless the will was drafted, "in contemplation of marriage".

- if you have a child after signing the will, it may be revoked if you have not dealt with this possibility in the will. If you are uncertain of the position in your state, check with a suitably qualified attorney in your state.

Appendices

Appendix 1

Glossary of Legal Terms

This glossary is designed to help you understand some of the more common legal terms you may encounter when making your will.

Term	Defintion
Administration	The process by which an administrator oversees the distribution of your estate and deals with the payment of any outstanding debts owing by you if you die intestate.
Administrator	This is the person who is designated by the courts to oversee the administration.
Adult	This is a person which has reached the age of majority in his or her state.
Assets	All possessions of yours including insurance policies and rights to receive other assets/money.
Beneficiary	A person or organization who will inherit part or all of your assets or estate under a will, trust or on intestacy.
Bequest	A gift of personal property under a will.
Children	The term extends to include legitimate, illegitimate and adopted children. Stepchildren are often excluded from the meaning of this term and should therefore, for the avoidance of doubt, be expressly mentioned in your will or trust if you wish them to benefit.
Codicil	A codicil acts to make an amendment to your will and is legally binding once all legal formalities have been complied with.

Deceased/Decedent   The person who has died.

Devise   This is a gift of immovable property (also known as real property) such as land or buildings made under a will.

Disinherit   To exclude someone who is rightfully entitled to inherit something from your estate from an inheritance.

Estate   The term "estate" refers to everything you own at the time of your death – all assets, real and personal, less your liabilities.

Executor/ Executrix   This is the person or persons nominated or appointed by you in your will to deal with the administration and distribution of your estate following your death. Executor is the masculine term whereas executrix is the feminine term. Sometimes, executors are called personal representatives.

Fiduciary   A fiduciary is someone who has undertaken to act for and on behalf of another person in a particular matter in circumstances which give rise to a relationship of trust and confidence. Examples include trustees, executors, and guardians.

Fiduciary Duty   Fiduciary duties are duties that the executor or trustee owes to the beneficiaries of the estate whose assets the executor or trustee has control over. These duties include a duty to act in good faith for the benefit of the beneficiaries.

Gift   A gift or a present is the transfer of something without the need for compensation and without any obligation on the part of the donor to make the gift.

Guardian   A legal guardian is a person who has the legal authority (and the corresponding duty) to care for the personal and property interests of a minor or an incapacitated person. In the case of minors, you can appoint a guardian under your will to care for your children following your death. However, this appointment must ultimately be approved by the court.

Heir
A person who is entitled either by law or by the terms of a will or trust to inherit the estate of another.

Inherit
To receive something, by legal succession or bequest, after the previous owner's death.

Intestate/Intestacy
Where you die without making a valid will to deal with the distribution of your estate you are said to have died intestate. Where this happens, intestacy proceedings will be instituted whereby the court will appoint an administrator to distribute your estate and pay your debts in accordance with the law. These laws are known as the rules of 'intestacy'.

Intestate Succession
The order in which people inherit property when someone dies intestate.

Issue
The immediate descendants of a person.

Legacy
A gift made in a will.

Minor
A child who has not yet reached the age of majority.

Per stirpes
A "per stirpes" arrangement means that if a beneficiary/heir predeceases the testator/intestate leaving a child then that child takes the share that his parent would have been entitled to receive had the parent been alive. Where there is more than one child, that share is divided equally amongst the children.

Personal Property
Physical assets that are not fixed permanently to real estate. It includes mobile property like furniture, equipment, vehicles, collectibles and inventory for example.

Personal Representative
Another name for an executor.

Primary Beneficiary	This is the person who stands first in line to receive a gift under a will or trust. Should the primary beneficiary die before becoming entitled to receive a gift under a will or trust, the gift will pass to an alternate beneficiary (if one is named) or revert to the residuary beneficiary if no alternate is named.
Probate	Probate has come to mean not just proving the validity of a last will and testament but the entire administrative process involving the collecting of assets, payment of debts and the passing of a deceased person's legal title to property to his or her beneficiaries. If the deceased person has not made a will, this process will be known as an administration rather than a probate.
Residue/Remainder	The remainder of a testator's estate after all specific gifts have been made under the testator's will, and after all of the testator's debts have been paid.
Residuary Beneficiary	The person who will receive the residue of the testator's estate. The residue can also be divided between more than one person.
Real Property	Land and generally whatever is erected upon or affixed to it.
Spouse	The person to whom you are married - not a cohabite.
Surviving Spouse	The husband or wife that remains alive after the death of the other spouse.
Survivorship	The right of a person to secure ownership of an asset (such as land, real estate, bank accounts etc.) by reason of the fact that this person has outlived the other joint owners.
Testamentary Trust	A trust created under the terms of a will.
Testate	A person who has died leaving a valid will providing for the distribution of his assets.
Testator/Testatrix	This means the man/woman who makes a will.

Trust

A trust is a relationship of reliance whereby one party requests another party to manage property on his or her behalf, or on behalf of another in accordance with a specific set of rules. The persons who are charged with the management of the property are known as trustees.

Trustee

The person or persons who have been appointed to look after property that is held in trust. The trustees are not allowed to do anything with the property unless the terms of the trust allow it. The trustees owe a number of fiduciary duties to the beneficiaries of the trust property concerned.

Will

A legal document setting out a person's wishes regarding the disposal of his or her property after death.

Appendix 2

Will Writing Worksheet

Downloadable Forms

Blank copies of this form can be downloaded from the EstateBee website. Simply login to your account or, if you don't have an account, you can create one for free.

www.estate-bee.com/login

Once logged in, go to your profile page and enter the code listed below in the 'Use Codes' tab:

Worksheet1492B

Will Writing Worksheet

Will Writing Worksheet

Before you begin the process of making a will, we recommend that you print out this worksheet and complete it as appropriate. It will help you to work out what assets you actually own, and identify your liabilities, before deciding who you would like to make gifts to and how. By having all the relevant details at your fingertips it will save a considerable amount of time in the preparation of your estate planning documents.

The document is also useful for documenting your choice of fiduciaries such as executors, trustees, healthcare agents, etc.

In addition, by keeping this worksheet with your will and other personal papers, it will greatly assist your executor in identifying and locating your assets and liabilities when the time comes.

Personal Information	You	Your Spouse
Full Name:		
Birth Date:		
Social Security Number:		
Occupation:		
Work Telephone:		
Work Fax:		
Mobile/Pager:		
Email Address:		
Home Address (Include County):		
Home Telephone:		
Home Fax:		

Date and Place of Marriage:	
Maiden name of Spouse:	

If either of you were previously married, list the dates of prior marriage, name of previous spouse, names of living children from prior marriage(s), and state whether marriage ended by death or divorce:		
Location of Safe Deposit Box (if any):		

Notification of Death

(On my death, please notify the following persons)

Full Name	Telephone	Address

Children (Living)		
Full Name	Address (if the child does not reside with you)	Birth Date

Children (Deceased)		
Full Name		

Grandchildren		
Full Name	Address	Birth Date

Parents		
Full Name	Address	Telephone Number

Brothers and Sisters		
Full Name	Address	Telephone Number

Assets		
Description & Location	Current Fair Market Value	How is Title Held?
Real Estate (Land and Buildings)		

Closely Held Companies, Businesses, Partnerships etc.		
Bank Accounts		
Shares, Bonds and Mutual Funds		
Vehicles, Boats, etc		

Other Property		
Total		

Liabilities

Description	Amount
Mortgages	
Loans	

Debts	
Other Liabilities	
Total	

Life Insurance and Annuities				
Company	Insured	Beneficiary(ies)	Face Amount	Cash Value
Total				

Pensions and Other Retirement Plans				
Company Custodian	Participant	Type of Plan	Vested Amount	Death Benefit
Total				

Distribution Plan
(Describe in general terms how you wish to leave your property at death)

Other Beneficiaries

(Information about persons other than your spouse and family members who you wish to benefit)

Full Name	Age	Address	Relationship to You

Fiduciaries

(List name, address and home telephone for each person)

	Full Name	Address	Telephone Number
Last Will and Testament			
Primary Executor:			
First Alternate Executor:			
Second Alternate Executor:			

Primary Trustee:			
First Alternate Trustee:			
Second Alternate Trustee:			
Guardian of Minor Children:			
First Alternate Guardian:			
Second Alternate Guardian:			
Living Trust			
Successor Trustee:			
First Alternate Successor Trustee:			
Second Alternate Successor Trustee:			
Agent under a Power of Attorney for Finance and Property			
Agent:			
First Alternate Agent:			
Second Alternate Agent:			
Agent under a Healthcare Power of Attorney			
Healthcare Agent:			

First Alternate Healthcare Agent:			
Second Alternate Healthcare Agent:			
Living Will			
Healthcare Agent:			
First Alternate Healthcare Agent:			
Second Alternate Healthcare Agent:			

Advisors

(List name, address and home telephone for each person)

	Full Name	Address	Telephone Number
Lawyer			
Accountant			
Financial Advisor			
Stockbroker			
Insurance Agent			
Other Information:			

Document Locations		
Description	Location	Other Information
Last Will & Testament		
Trust Agreement		
Living Will		
Healthcare Power of Attorney		
Power of Attorney for Finance and Property		
Title Deeds		
Leases		
Share Certificates		
Mortgage Documents		
Birth Certificate		
Marriage Certificate		
Divorce Decree		
Donor Cards		

Other Documents	

Funeral Plan

(Describe in general terms what funeral and burial arrangements you would like to have)

Appendix 3

Sample Wills

Appendix 3
Sample Wills

First Will & Second Will

Unmarried and not in a registered domestic partnership, with no children

These are "Simple Wills" and are used where a person is unmarried, and not in a registered domestic partnership and does not have any children. The will is used to appoint an executor and to pass your estate to designated persons of your choice.

The First Will should be used where you have one intended beneficiary for the residue of your estate.

The Second Will should be used where you have more than one intended beneficiary for the residue of your estate.

Third Will

Unmarried and not in a registered domestic partnership, with children

This will is for use by a person who is unmarried, not in a registered domestic partnership and has children. A trust will be created for the benefit of your children with power for the trustees to provide for your children until they reach a specific age (usually 18 to 21 years). Thereafter the residuary of your estate will be divided equally between your children.

Fourth Will & Fifth Will

Married or in a registered domestic partnership with adult children

These wills are for use by couples who are married or in a registered domestic partnership with adult children. In these wills, each spouse/partner leaves their estate to the other with a provision that, should the surviving spouse/partner die within a period of 30 days of the other spouse/partner, the entire estate will pass to a different named beneficiary.

The Fourth Will is for use by a husband or male partner. The Fifth Will is for use by a wife or female partner.

Sixth Will & Seventh Will

Married or in a registered domestic partnership with minor children

These wills are for use by a person who is married or in a registered domestic partnership and has minor children. In these wills, the spouse/partner leaves their estate to the other with a provision that, should they both die within a period of 30 days of each other the entire estate will pass to the trustees of the estate to hold the same on trust for the benefit of their minor children.

The Sixth Will is for use by a husband or male partner. The Seventh Will is for use by a wife or female partner.

Eighth Will & Ninth Will

Married or in a registered domestic partnership with no children

These wills are for use by a person who is married or in a registered domestic partnership and who does not have any living children. In these wills, the spouse/partner leaves their estate to the other with a provision that, should the surviving spouse/partner die within a period of 30 days of the other spouse/partner, the entire estate will pass to a different named beneficiary.

The Eighth Will is for use by a husband or male partner. The Ninth Will is for use by a wife or female partner.

FIRST WILL

(Person who is not married and not in a registered domestic partnership and has no children, single residuary beneficiary)

Downloadable Forms

Blank copies of this form can be downloaded from the EstateBee website. Simply login to your account or, if you don't have an account, you can create one for free.

www.estate-bee.com/login

Once logged in, go to your profile page and enter the code listed below in the 'Use Codes' tab:

FirstWill1492B

LAST WILL AND TESTAMENT

OF

_____

I, _____, of _____ in the State of _____, County of _____, being of sound and disposing mind and memory and having attained the age of majority in my state, hereby **REVOKE** all former wills, codicils and other testamentary dispositions at any time heretofore made by me and declare this to be my last will.

FIRST: I am not married, nor do I have a registered domestic partner. I do not have any living children.

SECOND: I appoint _____ of _____ to be executor of this my will. If this person or institution shall for any reason be unable or unwilling to act (at any time) as my executor, then I appoint _____ of _____ to be executor of my will. No executor appointed hereunder shall be required to post bond.

THIRD: I direct my executor to pay all my just debts (which are capable of enforcement against me), funeral and testamentary expenses as soon as practical after my death.

FOURTH: I give, devise, and bequeath _____ to _____ of ___ _____ absolutely.

FIFTH: I give, devise, and bequeath _____ to _____ of ____ _____ absolutely.

[Repeat or delete as necessary to make further specific gifts/bequests. Note you may need to renumber subsequent clauses]

SIXTH: As to all the rest, residue and remainder of my estate of whatsoever nature and wheresoever situate I give devise and bequeath the same to _____ of _____ _____. However, in the event that this person predeceases me or refuses to accept this gift, then I give devise and bequeath all the rest, residue and remainder of my estate to _____ of _____.

SEVENTH: In addition to all powers allowable to executors under the laws of this state, my executor shall have the following powers:

(a)   to dispose of any property or any interest therein at such times and upon such terms and conditions as shall seem proper and to give good and sufficient instruments of transfer and to receive the proceeds of any such disposition;

(b)   to purchase, manage, maintain and insure any property and to lease the same for such periods and on such terms as shall seem advantageous, and if advisable to pay for the value of any improvements made by a tenant under any such lease; to incur, extend or renew mortgage indebtedness; to make ordinary and extraordinary repairs and alterations to any building, to raze or erect buildings and to make improvements or to abandon any buildings or property; and to make any agreement of partition of such property and to give or receive money or other property in connection therewith;

(c)   to exercise or sell all rights, options, powers and privileges, and to vote in person or by proxy, in relation to any stocks, bonds or other securities, all as fully as might be done by persons owning similar property in their own right;

(d)   to manage, sell, administer, liquidate, continue or otherwise deal with any corporation, partnership or other business interest received by my trust estate as my executor deems fit;

(e)   to institute, defend, settle or compromise, by arbitration or otherwise, all claims;

(f)   to employ or retain such agents and advisors, including any firm with which any fiduciary may be affiliated, as may seem advisable and to delegate authority thereto, and to compensate them from the funds of my estate provided such compensation is reasonable in the circumstances;

(g)   to settle any entitlement of any beneficiary, in part or in whole, by payment in cash or by the transfer of a specific asset or assets to the beneficiary or to the legal guardian of the beneficiary with power to require the beneficiary or any such guardian to accept such asset or assets at such value or estimate of value as my executor shall (acting reasonably) unilaterally deem fair; and

(h)   to pay all necessary or proper expenses and charges from income or principal, or partly from each, in such manner as may seem equitable.

EIGHTH: To the extent that provision has not been made under this will for the management of any property, asset or item to be given outright to a person who is a minor, my executor may, without court approval, pay or transfer all or part of such property to a parent or guardian of that minor or that minor's estate, to a custodian under the Uniform Transfers to Minors Act, or may defer payment or transfer of such property until the minor reaches the age of majority, as defined by his or her state of residence. No bond shall be required for such payments.

NINTH: I declare that no executor of this will shall be liable for any loss not attributable to the executor's own dishonesty or to the wilful commission by the executor of any act known to be a breach of executor's duties and obligations as executor.

TENTH: If any person, whether or not related to me by blood or in any way, shall attempt, either directly or indirectly, to set aside the probate of my will or oppose or contest any of the provisions hereof, then any share or interest in my estate given to that person under my will shall be revoked and, in its stead, I give and bequeath the sum of one dollar ($1.00), only that, and no further interest whatever in my estate to such person.

IN WITNESS HEREOF, I sign the foregoing as my Last Will and Testament, do it willingly and as my free and voluntary act for the purpose herein expressed, this _____ day of _____ 20____.

_____
(Signed)

Signed by the above-named as and for his/her Last Will and Testament in our presence, each of us being present at the same time who at his/her request and in his/her presence and in the presence of each other have hereunto subscribed our names as witnesses.

We, the witnesses, sign our name to this document, and we declare under penalty of perjury, that the foregoing is true and correct, this _____ day of _____, 20____.

Name: _____

Signature: _____

Address: _____

_____

_____

_____

Name: _____

Signature: _____

Address: _____

_____

_____

_____

SECOND WILL

(Person who is not married and not in a registered domestic partnership and has no children, multiple beneficiaries)

Downloadable Forms

Blank copies of this form can be downloaded from the EstateBee website. Simply login to your account or, if you don't have an account, you can create one for free.

www.estate-bee.com/login

Once logged in, go to your profile page and enter the code listed below in the 'Use Codes' tab:

SecondWill1492B

LAST WILL AND TESTAMENT

OF

_____

I, _____, of _____ in the State of _____
_____, County of _____, being of sound and disposing mind
and memory and having attained the age of majority in my state, hereby **REVOKE** all former wills,
codicils and other testamentary dispositions at any time heretofore made by me and declare this to
be my last will.

FIRST: I am not married, nor do I have a registered domestic partner. I do not have any living
children.

SECOND: I appoint _____ of _____ to be executor of this
my will. If this person or institution shall for any reason be unable or unwilling to act (at any time)
as my executor, then I appoint _____ of _____ to be my
executor of my will. No executor appointed hereunder shall be required to post bond.

THIRD: I direct my executor to pay all my just debts (which are capable of enforcement against
me), funeral and testamentary expenses as soon as practical after my death.

FOURTH: I give, devise, and bequeath _____ to _____
_____ of _____ absolutely.

FIFTH: I give, devise, and bequeath _____ to _____
_ of _____ absolutely.

_[Repeat or delete as necessary to make further specific gifts/bequests. Note you may need to renumber
subsequent clauses]_

SIXTH: I give, devise, and bequeath all the rest, residue and remainder of my estate to _____
_____ of _____ and
_____ of _____ in equal shares. However,
in the event that either of the above persons predeceases me or refuses this gift, then I give, devise

and bequeath their share of my estate to _____ of _____
_____.

SEVENTH: In addition to all powers allowable to executors under the laws of this state, my executor shall have the following powers:

(a)   to dispose of any property or any interest therein at such times and upon such terms and conditions as shall seem proper and to give good and sufficient instruments of transfer and to receive the proceeds of any such disposition;

(b)   to purchase, manage, maintain and insure any property and to lease the same for such periods and on such terms as shall seem advantageous, and if advisable to pay for the value of any improvements made by a tenant under any such lease; to incur, extend or renew mortgage indebtedness; to make ordinary and extraordinary repairs and alterations to any building, to raze or erect buildings and to make improvements or to abandon any buildings or property; and to make any agreement of partition of such property and to give or receive money or other property in connection therewith;

(c)   to exercise or sell all rights, options, powers and privileges, and to vote in person or by proxy, in relation to any stocks, bonds or other securities, all as fully as might be done by persons owning similar property in their own right;

(d)   to manage, sell, administer, liquidate, continue or otherwise deal with any corporation, partnership or other business interest received by my trust estate as my Executor deems fit;

(e)   to institute, defend, settle or compromise, by arbitration or otherwise, all claims;

(f)   to employ or retain such agents and advisors, including any firm with which any fiduciary may be affiliated, as may seem advisable and to delegate authority thereto, and to compensate them from the funds of my estate provided such compensation is reasonable in the circumstances;

(g)   to settle any entitlement of any beneficiary, in part or in whole, by payment in cash or by the transfer of a specific asset or assets to the beneficiary or to the legal guardian of the beneficiary with power to require the beneficiary or any such guardian to accept such asset or assets at such value or estimate of value as my executor shall (acting reasonably) unilaterally deem fair; and

(h) to pay all necessary or proper expenses and charges from income or principal, or partly from each, in such manner as may seem equitable.

EIGHTH: To the extent that provision has not been made under the will for the management of any property, asset or item to be given outright to a person who is a minor, my executor may, without court approval, pay or transfer all or part of such property to a parent or guardian of that minor or that minor's estate, to a custodian under the Uniform Transfers to Minors Act, or may defer payment or transfer of such property until the minor reaches the age of majority, as defined by his or her state of residence. No bond shall be required for such payments.

NINTH: I declare that no executor of this will shall be liable for any loss not attributable to the executor's own dishonesty or to the wilful commission by the executor of any act known to be a breach of executor's duties and obligations as executor.

TENTH: If any person, whether or not related to me by blood or in any way, shall attempt, either directly or indirectly, to set aside the probate of my will or oppose or contest any of the provisions hereof, then any share or interest in my estate given to that person under my will shall be revoked and, in its stead, I give and bequeath the sum of one dollar ($1.00), only that, and no further interest whatever in my estate to such person.

IN WITNESS HEREOF, I sign the foregoing as my Last Will and Testament, do it willingly and as my free and voluntary act for the purpose herein expressed, this _____ day of _____ 20 ____.

_____
(Signed)

Signed by the above-named as and for his/her Last Will and Testament in our presence, each of us being present at the same time who at his/her request and in his/her presence and in the presence of each other have hereunto subscribed our names as witnesses.

We, the witnesses, sign our name to this document, and we declare under penalty of perjury, that the foregoing is true and correct, this _____ day of _____, 20 ____.

Name: _____

Signature: _____

Address: _____

_____

_____

_____

Name: _____

Signature: _____

Address: _____

_____

_____

_____

THIRD WILL

(Person who is not married and not in a registered domestic partnership and has children)

Downloadable Forms

Blank copies of all this form can be downloaded from the EstateBee website. Simply login to your account or, if you don't have an account, you can create one for free.

www.estate-bee.com/login

Once logged in, go to your profile page and enter the code listed below in the 'Use Codes' tab:

ThirdWill1492B

LAST WILL AND TESTAMENT

OF

_____

I, _____, of _____ in the State of _____ _____, County of _____, being of sound and disposing mind and memory and having attained the age of majority in my state, hereby **REVOKE** all former wills, codicils and other testamentary dispositions at any time heretofore made by me and declare this to be my last will.

FIRST: I am not married nor do I have a registered domestic partner. I have _____ child/children namely _____.

SECOND: I appoint _____ of _____ to be executor and trustee of this my will (my "Trustee"). If this person or institution shall for any reason be unable or unwilling to act (at any time) as my Trustee, then I appoint _____ of _____ to be my Trustee. No Trustee appointed hereunder shall be required to post bond.

THIRD: I direct my Trustee to pay all my just debts (which are capable of enforcement against me), funeral and testamentary expenses as soon as practical after my death.

FOURTH: I appoint _____ of _____ and _____ of _____ guardians of my infant children and conservators of the estate of each of my infant children, to serve as such without bond.

FIFTH: I give, devise, and bequeath _____ to _____ ___ of _____ absolutely.

SIXTH: I give, devise, and bequeath _____ to _____ of _____ absolutely.

[Repeat or delete as necessary to make further specific gifts/bequests. Note you may need to renumber subsequent clauses]

SEVENTH: I give, devise, and bequeath to my Trustee all the rest, residue and remainder of my estate upon trust to hold the same or the proceeds of sale thereof as trustee and to divide the same among such of my children as shall survive me and reach the age of _____ years and if more than one in equal shares absolutely BUT if any child of mine dies before me or before attaining a vested interest leaving a child or children then such child or children shall on reaching the age of _____ years take per stirpes the share which his/her parent would otherwise have taken and if more than one in equal shares absolutely.

EIGHTH: In addition to all powers allowable to executors under the laws of this state, my executor shall have the following powers:

(a) to dispose of any property or any interest therein at such times and upon such terms and conditions as shall seem proper and to give good and sufficient instruments of transfer and to receive the proceeds of any such disposition;

(b) to purchase, manage, maintain and insure any property and to lease the same for such periods and on such terms as shall seem advantageous, and if advisable to pay for the value of any improvements made by a tenant under any such lease; to incur, extend or renew mortgage indebtedness; to make ordinary and extraordinary repairs and alterations to any building, to raze or erect buildings and to make improvements or to abandon any buildings or property; and to make any agreement of partition of such property and to give or receive money or other property in connection therewith;

(c) to exercise or sell all rights, options, powers and privileges, and to vote in person or by proxy, in relation to any stocks, bonds or other securities, all as fully as might be done by persons owning similar property in their own right;

(d) to manage, sell, administer, liquidate, continue or otherwise deal with any corporation, partnership or other business interest received by my trust estate as my Executor deems fit;

(e) to institute, defend, settle or compromise, by arbitration or otherwise, all claims;

(f) to employ or retain such agents and advisors, including any firm with which any fiduciary may be affiliated, as may seem advisable and to delegate authority thereto, and to compensate them from the funds of my estate provided such compensation is reasonable in the circumstances;

(g) to settle any entitlement of any beneficiary, in part or in whole, by payment in cash or by the transfer of a specific asset or assets to the beneficiary or to the legal guardian of the beneficiary with power to require the beneficiary or any such guardian to accept such asset or assets at such value or estimate of value as my executor shall (acting reasonably) unilaterally deem fair; and

(h) to pay all necessary or proper expenses and charges from income or principal, or partly from each, in such manner as may seem equitable.

NINTH: In addition to all statutory powers and common law powers of gratuitous trustees, and special powers herein conferred, a trustee of an individual child trust shall have the fullest powers of investment, realisation, administration, management and division of the trust estate or any part thereof as if that trustee was the beneficial owner thereof; and, in particular, without prejudice to the generality of the foregoing, that trustee shall have the powers set out hereinafter:

(a) to receive from any person, to retain and to invest and reinvest in any kind of property or investment;

(b) to dispose of any property or any interest therein at such times and upon such terms and conditions as shall seem proper and to give good and sufficient instruments of transfer and to receive the proceeds of any such disposition;

(c) to purchase, manage, maintain and insure any property and to lease the same for such periods and on such terms as shall seem advantageous, and if advisable to pay for the value of any improvements made by a tenant under any such lease; to incur, extend or renew mortgage indebtedness; to make ordinary and extraordinary repairs and alterations to any building, to raze or erect buildings and to make improvements or to abandon any buildings or property; and to make any agreement of partition of such property and to give or receive money or other property in connection therewith;

(d) to exercise or sell all rights, options, powers and privileges, and to vote in person or by proxy, in relation to any stocks, bonds or other securities, all as fully as might be done by persons owning similar property in their own right;

(e) to assent to, oppose and participate in any reorganization, recapitalization, merger, consolidation or similar proceeding, to deposit securities, delegate discretionary powers, pay assessments or other expenses and exchange property, all as fully as might be done by persons owning similar property in their own right;

(f)   to manage, sell, administer, liquidate, continue or otherwise deal with any corporation, partnership or other business interest received by my trust estate as the trustee deems fit;

(g)   to borrow money and pledge or mortgage any property as security therefor;

(h)   to institute, defend, settle or compromise, by arbitration or otherwise, all claims;

(i)   to employ or retain such agents and advisors, including any firm with which any fiduciary may be affiliated, as may seem advisable and to delegate authority thereto, and to compensate them from the funds of my estate provided such compensation is reasonable in the circumstances; and

(j)   to pay all necessary or proper expenses and charges from income or principal, or partly from each, in such manner as may seem equitable.

TENTH: To the extent that provision has not been made under the will for the management of any property, asset or item to be given outright to a person who is a minor, my executor may, without court approval, pay or transfer all or part of such property to a parent or guardian of that minor or that minor's estate, to a custodian under the Uniform Transfers to Minors Act, or may defer payment or transfer of such property until the minor reaches the age of majority, as defined by his or her state of residence. No bond shall be required for such payments.

ELEVENTH: I declare that any executor and/or trustee for the time being a lawyer or other person engaged in any profession or business shall be entitled to charge and be paid all usual professional or other reasonable and proper charges for business done or services rendered or time spent by him or his firm in proving this will and administering my estate and in relation to the trusts of the will or of any codicil to it whether in the ordinary course of his profession or business or not and although not of a nature requiring the employment of a lawyer or other professional or business person.

TWELVETH: I declare that income received after my death shall be treated as income of my estate regardless of the period to which it relates.

THIRTEENTH: I declare that no advancement shall be brought into account in the distribution of my estate.

FOURTEENTH: I declare that no executor of this will shall be liable for any loss not attributable to the executor's own dishonesty or to the wilful commission by the executor of any act known to be a breach of executor's duties and obligations as executor.

FIFTEENTH: If any person, whether or not related to me by blood or in any way, shall attempt, either directly or indirectly, to set aside the probate of my will or oppose or contest any of the provisions hereof, then any share or interest in my estate given to that person under my will shall be revoked and, in its stead, I give and bequeath the sum of one dollar ($1.00), only that, and no further interest whatever in my estate to such person.

IN WITNESS HEREOF, I sign the foregoing as my Last Will and Testament, do it willingly and as my free and voluntary act for the purpose herein expressed, this _____ day of _____ 20 ____.

_____
(Signed)

Signed by the above-named as and for his/her Last Will and Testament in our presence, each of us being present at the same time who at his/her request and in his/her presence and in the presence of each other have hereunto subscribed our names as witnesses.

We, the witnesses, sign our name to this document, and we declare under penalty of perjury, that the foregoing is true and correct, this _____ day of _____, 20 ____.

Name: _____

Signature: _____

Address: _____

_____

_____

_____

Name: _____

Signature: _____

Address: _____

_____

_____

FOURTH WILL

(Married or in a registered domestic partnership with adult children (for husband/male partner))

Downloadable Forms

Blank copies of this form can be downloaded from the EstateBee website. Simply login to your account or, if you don't have an account, you can create one for free.

www.estate-bee.com/login

Once logged in, go to your profile page and enter the code listed below in the 'use code' tab:

FourthWill1492B

LAST WILL AND TESTAMENT

OF

_____

I, _____, of _____ in the State
of _____, County of _____, being of sound
and disposing mind and memory and having attained the age of majority in my state, hereby
REVOKE all former wills, codicils and other testamentary dispositions at any time heretofore
made by me and declare this to be my last will.

FIRST: [I am married to _____.]/[I am in a registered domestic partnership
with _____.] I have _____ child/children namely _____
___.

SECOND: I appoint _____ of _____ to be executor of this
my will. If this person or institution shall for any reason be unable or unwilling to act (at any time)
as my executor, then I appoint _____ of _____ to be my
executor of my will. No executor appointed hereunder shall be required to post bond.

THIRD: I direct my executor to pay all my just debts (which are capable of enforcement against
me), funeral and testamentary expenses as soon as practical after my death.

FOURTH: I give, devise, and bequeath _____ to _____
_____ of _____ absolutely.

FIFTH: I give, devise, and bequeath _____ to _____
_____ of _____ absolutely.

*[Repeat or delete as necessary to make further specific gifts/bequests. Note you may need to renumber
subsequent clauses]*

SIXTH: If my [spouse]/[partner], _____, shall survive me for a period of
one month then **I GIVE, DEVISE AND BEQUEATH** all the rest, residue and remainder of my estate

of whatsoever kind and wheresoever situate to my said [spouse]/[partner] absolutely.

SEVENTH: If my said [spouse]/[partner] shall predecease me or shall not survive me for the period aforesaid I DIRECT that the previous clause shall not take effect and this my will shall be construed and take effect as if the previous clause had been wholly omitted therefrom and that the remaining clauses of this will shall take effect.

EIGHTH: In so far as it may be necessary and for the avoidance of doubt I direct that if my [spouse]/[partner] shall survive me for a period of less than one month then the income of my estate accruing from the date of my death until the date of the death of my [spouse]/[partner] shall be accumulated and form part of my residuary estate.

NINTH: I give, devise, and bequeath all the rest, residue and remainder of my estate to _____ _____ of _____ and _____ _____ of _____in equal shares. However, in the event that either of the above persons predeceases me or refuses this gift, then I give, devise and bequeath their share of my estate to _____ of _____.

TENTH: In addition to all powers allowable to executors under the laws of this state, my executor shall have the following powers:

(a) to dispose of any property or any interest therein at such times and upon such terms and conditions as shall seem proper and to give good and sufficient instruments of transfer and to receive the proceeds of any such disposition;

(b) to purchase, manage, maintain and insure any property and to lease the same for such periods and on such terms as shall seem advantageous, and if advisable to pay for the value of any improvements made by a tenant under any such lease; to incur, extend or renew mortgage indebtedness; to make ordinary and extraordinary repairs and alterations to any building, to raze or erect buildings and to make improvements or to abandon any buildings or property; and to make any agreement of partition of such property and to give or receive money or other property in connection therewith;

(c) to exercise or sell all rights, options, powers and privileges, and to vote in person or by proxy, in relation to any stocks, bonds or other securities, all as fully as might be done by persons owning similar property in their own right;

(d) to manage, sell, administer, liquidate, continue or otherwise deal with any corporation, partnership or other business interest received by my trust estate as my Executor deems fit;

(e) to institute, defend, settle or compromise, by arbitration or otherwise, all claims;

(f) to employ or retain such agents and advisors, including any firm with which any fiduciary may be affiliated, as may seem advisable and to delegate authority thereto, and to compensate them from the funds of my estate provided such compensation is reasonable in the circumstances;

(g) to settle any entitlement of any beneficiary, in part or in whole, by payment in cash or by the transfer of a specific asset or assets to the beneficiary or to the legal guardian of the beneficiary with power to require the beneficiary or any such guardian to accept such asset or assets at such value or estimate of value as my executor shall (acting reasonably) unilaterally deem fair; and

(h) to pay all necessary or proper expenses and charges from income or principal, or partly from each, in such manner as may seem equitable.

ELEVENTH: To the extent that provision has not been made under the will for the management of any property, asset or item to be given outright to a person who is a minor, my executor may, without court approval, pay or transfer all or part of such property to a parent or guardian of that minor or that minor's estate, to a custodian under the Uniform Transfers to Minors Act, or may defer payment or transfer of such property until the minor reaches the age of majority, as defined by his or her state of residence. No bond shall be required for such payments.

TWELVETH: I declare that any executor and/or trustee for the time being a lawyer or other person engaged in any profession or business shall be entitled to charge and be paid all usual professional or other reasonable and proper charges for business done or services rendered or time spent by him or his firm in proving this will and administering my estate and in relation to the trusts of the will or of any codicil to it whether in the ordinary course of his profession or business or not and although not of a nature requiring the employment of a lawyer or other professional or business person.

THIRTEENTH: I declare that income received after my death shall be treated as income of my estate regardless of the period to which it relates.

FOURTEENTH: I declare that no executor of this will shall be liable for any loss not attributable to the executor's own dishonesty or to the wilful commission by the executor of any act known to be a breach of executor's duties and obligations as executor.

FIFTEENTH: If any person, whether or not related to me by blood or in any way, shall attempt, either directly or indirectly, to set aside the probate of my will or oppose or contest any of the provisions hereof, then any share or interest in my estate given to that person under my will shall be revoked and, in its stead, I give and bequeath the sum of one dollar ($1.00), only that, and no further interest whatever in my estate to such person.

IN WITNESS HEREOF, I sign the foregoing as my Last Will and Testament, do it willingly and as my free and voluntary act for the purpose herein expressed, this ___ day of _____ 20 _____.

_____
(Signed)

Signed by the above-named as and for his Last Will and Testament in our presence, each of us being present at the same time who at his request and in his presence and in the presence of each other have hereunto subscribed our names as witnesses.

We, the witnesses, sign our name to this document, and we declare under penalty of perjury, that the foregoing is true and correct, this _____ day of _____, 20___.

Name: _____
Signature: _____
Address: _____
_____
_____
_____

Name: _____
Signature: _____
Address: _____
_____
_____

FIFTH WILL

(Married or in a registered domestic partnership with adult children (for wife/female partner))

Downloadable Forms

Blank copies of this form can be downloaded from the EstateBee website. Simply login to your account or, if you don't have an account, you can create one for free.

www.estate-bee.com/login

Once logged in, go to your profile page and enter the code listed below in the 'Use Codes' tab:

FifthWill1492B

LAST WILL AND TESTAMENT

OF

_____

I, _____, of _____ in the State of __
_____, County of _____, being of sound and
disposing mind and memory and having attained the age of majority in my state, hereby **REVOKE**
all former wills, codicils and other testamentary dispositions at any time heretofore made by me
and declare this to be my last will.

FIRST: [I am married to _____.]/[I am in a registered domestic partnership
_____.] I have _____ child/children namely _____.

SECOND: I appoint _____ of _____ to be executor of this my
will. If this person or institution shall for any reason be unable or unwilling to act (at any time) as
my executor, then I appoint _____ of _____ to be my executor of
my will. No executor appointed hereunder shall be required to post bond.

THIRD: I direct my executor to pay all my just debts (which are capable of enforcement against
me), funeral and testamentary expenses as soon as practical after my death.

FOURTH: I give, devise, and bequeath _____ to _____
_____ of _____ absolutely.

FIFTH: I give, devise, and bequeath _____ to _____
_____ of _____ absolutely.

_[Repeat or delete as necessary to make further specific gifts/bequests. Note you may need to renumber
subsequent clauses]_

SIXTH: If my [spouse]/[partner], _____, shall survive me for a period of
one month then **I GIVE, DEVISE AND BEQUEATH** all the rest, residue and remainder of my estate
of whatsoever kind and wheresoever situate to my said [spouse]/[partner] absolutely.

SEVENTH: If my said [spouse]/[partner] shall predecease me or shall not survive me for the period aforesaid **I DIRECT** that the previous clause shall not take effect and this my will shall be construed and take effect as if the previous clause had been wholly omitted therefrom and that the remaining clauses of this will shall take effect.

EIGHTH: In so far as it may be necessary and for the avoidance of doubt I direct that if my [spouse]/[partner] shall survive me for a period of less than one month then the income of my estate accruing from the date of my death until the date of the death of my [spouse]/[partner] shall be accumulated and form part of my residuary estate.

NINTH: I give, devise, and bequeath all the rest, residue and remainder of my estate to _____ of _____ and ___ _____ of _____in equal shares. However, in the event that either of the above persons predeceases me or refuses this gift, then I give, devise and bequeath their share of my estate to _____ of _____ _____.

TENTH: In addition to all powers allowable to executors under the laws of this state, my executor shall have the following powers:

(a)   to dispose of any property or any interest therein at such times and upon such terms and conditions as shall seem proper and to give good and sufficient instruments of transfer and to receive the proceeds of any such disposition;

(b)   to purchase, manage, maintain and insure any property and to lease the same for such periods and on such terms as shall seem advantageous, and if advisable to pay for the value of any improvements made by a tenant under any such lease; to incur, extend or renew mortgage indebtedness; to make ordinary and extraordinary repairs and alterations to any building, to raze or erect buildings and to make improvements or to abandon any buildings or property; and to make any agreement of partition of such property and to give or receive money or other property in connection therewith;

(c)   to exercise or sell all rights, options, powers and privileges, and to vote in person or by proxy, in relation to any stocks, bonds or other securities, all as fully as might be done by persons owning similar property in their own right;

(d)   to manage, sell, administer, liquidate, continue or otherwise deal with any corporation, partnership or other business interest received by my trust estate as my Executor deems fit;

(e)   to institute, defend, settle or compromise, by arbitration or otherwise, all claims;

(f)   to employ or retain such agents and advisors, including any firm with which any fiduciary may be affiliated, as may seem advisable and to delegate authority thereto, and to compensate them from the funds of my estate provided such compensation is reasonable in the circumstances;

(g)   to settle any entitlement of any beneficiary, in part or in whole, by payment in cash or by the transfer of a specific asset or assets to the beneficiary or to the legal guardian of the beneficiary with power to require the beneficiary or any such guardian to accept such asset or assets at such value or estimate of value as my executor shall (acting reasonably) unilaterally deem fair; and

(h)   to pay all necessary or proper expenses and charges from income or principal, or partly from each, in such manner as may seem equitable.

ELEVENTH: To the extent that provision has not been made under the will for the management of any property, asset or item to be given outright to a person who is a minor, my executor may, without court approval, pay or transfer all or part of such property to a parent or guardian of that minor or that minor's estate, to a custodian under the Uniform Transfers to Minors Act, or may defer payment or transfer of such property until the minor reaches the age of majority, as defined by his or her state of residence. No bond shall be required for such payments.

TWELVETH: I declare that any executor and/or trustee for the time being a lawyer or other person engaged in any profession or business shall be entitled to charge and be paid all usual professional or other reasonable and proper charges for business done or services rendered or time spent by him or his firm in proving this will and administering my estate and in relation to the trusts of the will or of any codicil to it whether in the ordinary course of his profession or business or not and although not of a nature requiring the employment of a lawyer or other professional or business person.

THIRTEENTH: I declare that income received after my death shall be treated as income of my estate regardless of the period to which it relates.

FOURTEENTH: I declare that no executor of this will shall be liable for any loss not attributable to the executor's own dishonesty or to the wilful commission by the executor of any act known to be a breach of executor's duties and obligations as executor.

FIFTEENTH: If any person, whether or not related to me by blood or in any way, shall attempt, either directly or indirectly, to set aside the probate of my will or oppose or contest any of the provisions hereof, then any share or interest in my estate given to that person under my will shall be revoked and, in its stead, I give and bequeath the sum of one dollar ($1.00), only that, and no further interest whatever in my estate to such person.

IN WITNESS HEREOF, I sign the foregoing as my Last Will and Testament, do it willingly and as my free and voluntary act for the purpose herein expressed, this _____ day of _____ 20_____.

_____
(Signed)

Signed by the above-named as and for her Last Will and Testament in our presence, each of us being present at the same time who at her request and in her presence and in the presence of each other have hereunto subscribed our names as witnesses.

We, the witnesses, sign our name to this document, and we declare under penalty of perjury, that the foregoing is true and correct, this _____ day of _____, 20_____.

Name: _____

Signature: _____

Address: _____

_____

_____

_____

Name: _____

Signature: _____

Address: _____

_____

_____

_____

SIXTH WILL

(Married or in a registered domestic partnership with minor children (for husband/male partner))

Downloadable Forms

Blank copies of this form can be downloaded from the EstateBee website. Simply login to your account or, if you don't have an account, you can create one for free.

www.estate-bee.com/login

Once logged in, go to your profile page and enter the code listed below in the 'Use Codes' tab:

SixthWill1492B

LAST WILL AND TESTAMENT

OF

_____

I, _____, of _____ in the State of _____
_____, County of _____, being of sound and disposing
mind and memory and having attained the age of majority in my state, hereby **REVOKE** all former
wills, codicils and other testamentary dispositions at any time heretofore made by me and declare
this to be my last will.

FIRST: [I am married to _____.]/[I am in a registered domestic partnership
_____.] I have ____ child/children namely _____.

SECOND: I appoint _____ of _____ to be executor and trustee
of this my will (my "Trustee"). If this person or institution shall for any reason be unable or
unwilling to act (at any time) as my Trustee, then I appoint
_____ of _____ to be my Trustee. No Trustee
appointed hereunder shall be required to post bond.

THIRD: I direct my Trustee to pay all my just debts (which are capable of enforcement against me),
funeral and testamentary expenses as soon as practical after my death.

FOURTH: I appoint _____ of _____ and _____
_____ of _____ guardians of my infant children and conservators of
the estate of each of my infant children, to serve as such without bond.

FIFTH: I give, devise, and bequeath _____ to
_____ of _____ absolutely.

SIXTH: I give, devise, and bequeath _____ to
_____ of _____ absolutely.

_[Repeat or delete as necessary to make further specific gifts/bequests. Note you may need to renumber
subsequent clauses]_

SEVENTH: If my [spouse]/[partner], _____, shall survive me for a period of one month then **I GIVE, DEVISE AND BEQUEATH** all the rest, residue and remainder of my estate of whatsoever kind and wheresoever situate to my said [spouse]/[partner] absolutely.

EIGHTH: If my said [spouse]/[partner] shall predecease me or shall not survive me for the period aforesaid **I DIRECT** that the previous clause shall not take effect and this my will shall be construed and take effect as if the previous clause had been wholly omitted therefrom and that the remaining clauses of this will shall take effect.

NINTH: In so far as it may be necessary and for the avoidance of doubt I direct that if my [spouse]/[partner] shall survive me for a period of less than one month then the income of my estate accruing from the date of my death until the date of the death of my [wife]/[partner] shall be accumulated and form part of my residuary estate.

TENTH: I give, devise, and bequeath to my Trustee all the rest, residue and remainder of my estate upon trust to hold the same or the proceeds of sale thereof as trustee and to divide the same among such of my children as shall survive me and reach the age of _____ years and if more than one in equal shares absolutely BUT if any child of mine dies before me or before attaining a vested interest leaving a child or children then such child or children shall on reaching the age of _____ years take per stirpes the share which his/her parent would otherwise have taken and if more than one in equal shares absolutely.

ELEVENTH: In addition to all powers allowable to executors under the laws of this state, my executor shall have the following powers:

(a) to dispose of any property or any interest therein at such times and upon such terms and conditions as shall seem proper and to give good and sufficient instruments of transfer and to receive the proceeds of any such disposition;

(b) to purchase, manage, maintain and insure any property and to lease the same for such periods and on such terms as shall seem advantageous, and if advisable to pay for the value of any improvements made by a tenant under any such lease; to incur, extend or renew mortgage indebtedness; to make ordinary and extraordinary repairs and alterations to any building, to raze or erect buildings and to make improvements or to abandon any buildings or property; and to make any agreement of partition of such property and to give or receive money or other property in connection therewith;

(c) to exercise or sell all rights, options, powers and privileges, and to vote in person or by proxy, in relation to any stocks, bonds or other securities, all as fully as might be done by persons owning similar property in their own right;

(d) to manage, sell, administer, liquidate, continue or otherwise deal with any corporation, partnership or other business interest received by my trust estate as my Executor deems fit;

(e) to institute, defend, settle or compromise, by arbitration or otherwise, all claims;

(f) to employ or retain such agents and advisors, including any firm with which any fiduciary may be affiliated, as may seem advisable and to delegate authority thereto, and to compensate them from the funds of my estate provided such compensation is reasonable in the circumstances;

(g) to settle any entitlement of any beneficiary, in part or in whole, by payment in cash or by the transfer of a specific asset or assets to the beneficiary or to the legal guardian of the beneficiary with power to require the beneficiary or any such guardian to accept such asset or assets at such value or estimate of value as my executor shall (acting reasonably) unilaterally deem fair; and

(h) to pay all necessary or proper expenses and charges from income or principal, or partly from each, in such manner as may seem equitable.

TWELFTH: In addition to all statutory powers and common law powers of gratuitous trustees, and special powers herein conferred, a trustee of an individual child trust shall have the fullest powers of investment, realisation, administration, management and division of the trust estate or any part thereof as if that trustee was the beneficial owner thereof; and, in particular, without prejudice to the generality of the foregoing, that trustee shall have the powers set out hereinafter:

(a) to receive from any person, to retain and to invest and reinvest in any kind of property or investment;

(b) to dispose of any property or any interest therein at such times and upon such terms and conditions as shall seem proper and to give good and sufficient instruments of transfer and to receive the proceeds of any such disposition;

(c) to purchase, manage, maintain and insure any property and to lease the same for such periods and on such terms as shall seem advantageous, and if advisable to pay for the value of any improvements made by a tenant under any such lease; to incur, extend or renew mortgage indebtedness; to make ordinary and extraordinary repairs and alterations to any building, to raze or erect buildings and to make improvements or to abandon any buildings or property; and to make any agreement of partition of such property and to give or receive money or other property in connection therewith;

(d) to exercise or sell all rights, options, powers and privileges, and to vote in person or by proxy, in relation to any stocks, bonds or other securities, all as fully as might be done by persons owning similar property in their own right;

(e) to assent to, oppose and participate in any reorganization, recapitalization, merger, consolidation or similar proceeding, to deposit securities, delegate discretionary powers, pay assessments or other expenses and exchange property, all as fully as might be done by persons owning similar property in their own right;

(f) to manage, sell, administer, liquidate, continue or otherwise deal with any corporation, partnership or other business interest received by my trust estate as the trustee deems fit;

(g) to borrow money and pledge or mortgage any property as security therefor;

(h) to institute, defend, settle or compromise, by arbitration or otherwise, all claims;

(i) to employ or retain such agents and advisors, including any firm with which any fiduciary may be affiliated, as may seem advisable and to delegate authority thereto, and to compensate them from the funds of my estate provided such compensation is reasonable in the circumstances; and

(j) to pay all necessary or proper expenses and charges from income or principal, or partly from each, in such manner as may seem equitable.

THIRTEENTH: To the extent that provision has not been made under the will for the management of any property, asset or item to be given outright to a person who is a minor, my executor may, without court approval, pay or transfer all or part of such property to a parent or guardian of that minor or that minor's estate, to a custodian under the Uniform Transfers to Minors Act, or may defer payment or transfer of such property until the minor reaches the age of majority, as defined by his or her state of residence. No bond shall be required for such payments.

FOURTEENTH: I declare that any executor and/or trustee for the time being a lawyer or other person engaged in any profession or business shall be entitled to charge and be paid all usual professional or other reasonable and proper charges for business done or services rendered or time spent by him or his firm in proving this will and administering my estate and in relation to the trusts of the will or of any codicil to it whether in the ordinary course of his profession or business or not and although not of a nature requiring the employment of a lawyer or other professional or business person.

FIFTEENTH: I declare that income received after my death shall be treated as income of my estate regardless of the period to which it relates.

SIXTEENTH: I declare that no advancement shall be brought into account in the distribution of my estate.

SEVENTEENTH: I declare that no executor of this will shall be liable for any loss not attributable to the executor's own dishonesty or to the wilful commission by the executor of any act known to be a breach of executor's duties and obligations as executor.

EIGHTEENTH: If any person, whether or not related to me by blood or in any way, shall attempt, either directly or indirectly, to set aside the probate of my will or oppose or contest any of the provisions hereof, then any share or interest in my estate given to that person under my will shall be revoked and, in its stead, I give and bequeath the sum of one dollar ($1.00), only that, and no further interest whatever in my estate to such person.

IN WITNESS HEREOF, I sign the foregoing as my Last Will and Testament, do it willingly and as my free and voluntary act for the purpose herein expressed, this _____ day of _____ 20_____.

_____
(Signed)

Signed by the above-named as and for his Last Will and Testament in our presence, each of us being present at the same time who at his request and in his presence and in the presence of each other have hereunto subscribed our names as witnesses.

We, the witnesses, sign our name to this document, and we declare under penalty of perjury, that the foregoing is true and correct, this _____ day of _____, 20__.

Name: _____

Signature: _____

Address: _____

_____

_____

_____

Name: _____

Signature: _____

Address: _____

_____

_____

_____

SEVENTH WILL

(Married or in a registered domestic partnership with minor children (for wife/female partner))

Downloadable Forms

Blank copies of this form can be downloaded from the EstateBee website. Simply login to your account or, if you don't have an account, you can create one for free.

www.estate-bee.com/login

Once logged in, go to your profile page and enter the code listed below in the 'Use Codes' tab:

SeventhWill1492B

LAST WILL AND TESTAMENT

OF

_____

I, _____, of _____ in the State of _____, County of _____, being of sound and disposing mind and memory and having attained the age of majority in my state, hereby **REVOKE** all former wills, codicils and other testamentary dispositions at any time heretofore made by me and declare this to be my last will.

FIRST: [I am married to _____.]/[I am in a registered domestic partnership with_____.] I have _____ child/children namely _____.

SECOND: I appoint _____ of _____ to be executor and trustee of this my will (my "Trustee"). If this person or institution shall for any reason be unable or unwilling to act (at any time) as my Trustee, then I appoint _____ of _____ to be my Trustee. No Trustee appointed hereunder shall be required to post bond.

THIRD: I direct my Trustee to pay all my just debts (which are capable of enforcement against me), funeral and testamentary expenses as soon as practical after my death.

FOURTH: I appoint _____ of _____ and _____ _____ of _____ guardians of my infant children and conservators of the estate of each of my infant children, to serve as such without bond.

FIFTH: I give, devise, and bequeath _____ to _____ of _____ absolutely.

SIXTH: I give, devise, and bequeath _____ to _____ of _____ absolutely.

[Repeat or delete as necessary to make further specific gifts/bequests. Note you may need to renumber subsequent clauses]

SEVENTH: If my [spouse]/[partner], _____, shall survive me for a period of one month then **I GIVE, DEVISE AND BEQUEATH** all the rest, residue and remainder of my estate of whatsoever kind and wheresoever situate to my said [spouse]/[partner] absolutely.

EIGHTH: If my said [spouse]/[partner] shall predecease me or shall not survive me for the period aforesaid **I DIRECT** that the previous clause shall not take effect and this my will shall be construed and take effect as if the previous clause had been wholly omitted therefrom and that the remaining clauses of this will shall take effect.

NINTH: In so far as it may be necessary and for the avoidance of doubt I direct that if my [spouse]/[partner] shall survive me for a period of less than one month then the income of my estate accruing from the date of my death until the date of the death of my [spouse]/[partner] shall be accumulated and form part of my residuary estate.

TENTH: I give, devise, and bequeath to my Trustee all the rest, residue and remainder of my estate upon trust to hold the same or the proceeds of sale thereof as trustee and to divide the same among such of my children as shall survive me and reach the age of _____ _ years and if more than one in equal shares absolutely BUT if any child of mine dies before me or before attaining a vested interest leaving a child or children then such child or children shall on reaching the age of _____ years take per stirpes the share which his/her parent would otherwise have taken and if more than one in equal shares absolutely.

ELEVENTH: In addition to all powers allowable to executors under the laws of this state, my executor shall have the following powers:

(a) to dispose of any property or any interest therein at such times and upon such terms and conditions as shall seem proper and to give good and sufficient instruments of transfer and to receive the proceeds of any such disposition;

(b) to purchase, manage, maintain and insure any property and to lease the same for such periods and on such terms as shall seem advantageous, and if advisable to pay for the value of any improvements made by a tenant under any such lease; to incur, extend or renew mortgage indebtedness; to make ordinary and extraordinary repairs and alterations to any building, to raze or erect buildings and to make improvements or to abandon any buildings or property; and to make any agreement of partition of such property and to give or receive money or other property in connection therewith;

(c) to exercise or sell all rights, options, powers and privileges, and to vote in person or by proxy, in relation to any stocks, bonds or other securities, all as fully as might be done by persons owning similar property in their own right;

(d) to manage, sell, administer, liquidate, continue or otherwise deal with any corporation, partnership or other business interest received by my trust estate as my Executor deems fit;

(e) to institute, defend, settle or compromise, by arbitration or otherwise, all claims;

(f) to employ or retain such agents and advisors, including any firm with which any fiduciary may be affiliated, as may seem advisable and to delegate authority thereto, and to compensate them from the funds of my estate provided such compensation is reasonable in the circumstances;

(g) to settle any entitlement of any beneficiary, in part or in whole, by payment in cash or by the transfer of a specific asset or assets to the beneficiary or to the legal guardian of the beneficiary with power to require the beneficiary or any such guardian to accept such asset or assets at such value or estimate of value as my executor shall (acting reasonably) unilaterally deem fair; and

(h) to pay all necessary or proper expenses and charges from income or principal, or partly from each, in such manner as may seem equitable.

TWELFTH: In addition to all statutory powers and common law powers of gratuitous trustees, and special powers herein conferred, a trustee of an individual child trust shall have the fullest powers of investment, realisation, administration, management and division of the trust estate or any part thereof as if that trustee was the beneficial owner thereof; and, in particular, without prejudice to the generality of the foregoing, that trustee shall have the powers set out hereinafter:

(a) to receive from any person, to retain and to invest and reinvest in any kind of property or investment;

(b) to dispose of any property or any interest therein at such times and upon such terms and conditions as shall seem proper and to give good and sufficient instruments of transfer and to receive the proceeds of any such disposition;

(c) to purchase, manage, maintain and insure any property and to lease the same for such periods and on such terms as shall seem advantageous, and if advisable to pay for the value of any improvements made by a tenant under any such lease; to incur, extend or renew mortgage indebtedness; to make ordinary and extraordinary repairs and alterations to any building, to raze or erect buildings and to make improvements or to abandon any buildings or property; and to make any agreement of partition of such property and to give or receive money or other property in connection therewith;

(d) to exercise or sell all rights, options, powers and privileges, and to vote in person or by proxy, in relation to any stocks, bonds or other securities, all as fully as might be done by persons owning similar property in their own right;

(e) to assent to, oppose and participate in any reorganization, recapitalization, merger, consolidation or similar proceeding, to deposit securities, delegate discretionary powers, pay assessments or other expenses and exchange property, all as fully as might be done by persons owning similar property in their own right;

(f) to manage, sell, administer, liquidate, continue or otherwise deal with any corporation, partnership or other business interest received by my trust estate as the trustee deems fit;

(g) to borrow money and pledge or mortgage any property as security therefor;

(h) to institute, defend, settle or compromise, by arbitration or otherwise, all claims;

(i) to employ or retain such agents and advisors, including any firm with which any fiduciary may be affiliated, as may seem advisable and to delegate authority thereto, and to compensate them from the funds of my estate provided such compensation is reasonable in the circumstances; and

(j) to pay all necessary or proper expenses and charges from income or principal, or partly from each, in such manner as may seem equitable.

THIRTEENTH: To the extent that provision has not been made under the will for the management of any property, asset or item to be given outright to a person who is a minor, my executor may, without court approval, pay or transfer all or part of such property to a parent or guardian of that minor or that minor's estate, to a custodian under the Uniform Transfers to Minors Act, or may defer payment or transfer of such property until the minor reaches the age of majority, as defined by his or her state of residence. No bond shall be required for such payments.

FOURTEENTH: I declare that any executor and/or trustee for the time being a lawyer or other person engaged in any profession or business shall be entitled to charge and be paid all usual professional or other reasonable and proper charges for business done or services rendered or time spent by him or his firm in proving this will and administering my estate and in relation to the trusts of the will or of any codicil to it whether in the ordinary course of his profession or business or not and although not of a nature requiring the employment of a lawyer or other professional or business person.

FIFTEENTH: I declare that income received after my death shall be treated as income of my estate regardless of the period to which it relates.

SIXTEENTH: I declare that no advancement shall be brought into account in the distribution of my estate.

SEVENTEENTH: I declare that no executor of this will shall be liable for any loss not attributable to the executor's own dishonesty or to the wilful commission by the executor of any act known to be a breach of executor's duties and obligations as executor.

EIGHTEENTH: If any person, whether or not related to me by blood or in any way, shall attempt, either directly or indirectly, to set aside the probate of my will or oppose or contest any of the provisions hereof, then any share or interest in my estate given to that person under my will shall be revoked and, in its stead, I give and bequeath the sum of one dollar ($1.00), only that, and no further interest whatever in my estate to such person.

IN WITNESS HEREOF, I sign the foregoing as my Last Will and Testament, do it willingly and as my free and voluntary act for the purpose herein expressed, this _____ day of
_____ 20_____.

_____
(Signed)

Signed by the above-named as and for her Last Will and Testament in our presence, each of us being present at the same time who at her request and in her presence and in the presence of each other have hereunto subscribed our names as witnesses.

We, the witnesses, sign our name to this document, and we declare under penalty of perjury, that the foregoing is true and correct, this _____ day of _____, 20____.

Name: _____

Signature: _____

Address: _____

_____

_____

_____

Name: _____

Signature: _____

Address: _____

_____

_____

_____

EIGHTH WILL

(Married or in a registered domestic partnership with no children (for husband/male partner))

Downloadable Forms

Blank copies of this form can be downloaded from the EstateBee website. Simply login to your account or, if you don't have an account, you can create one for free.

www.estate-bee.com/login

Once logged in, go to your profile page and enter the code listed below in the 'Use Codes' tab:

EighthWill1492B

LAST WILL AND TESTAMENT

OF

_____

I, _____, of _____ in the State of _____ _____, County of _____, being of sound and disposing mind and memory and having attained the age of majority in my state, hereby **REVOKE** all former wills, codicils and other testamentary dispositions at any time heretofore made by me and declare this to be my last will.

FIRST: [I am married to _____.]/[I am in a registered domestic partnership with _____.] I do not have any living children.

SECOND: I appoint _____ of _____ to be executor of this my will. If this person or institution shall for any reason be unable or unwilling to act (at any time) as my executor, then I appoint _____of _____ to be my executor of my will. No executor appointed hereunder shall be required to post bond.

THIRD: I direct my executor to pay all my just debts (which are capable of enforcement against me), funeral and testamentary expenses as soon as practical after my death.

FOURTH: I give, devise, and bequeath _____ to _____ of _____ absolutely.

FIFTH: I give, devise, and bequeath _____ to _____ of ___ _____ absolutely.

[Repeat or delete as necessary to make further specific gifts/bequests. Note you may need to renumber subsequent clauses]

SIXTH: If my [spouse]/[partner], _____, shall survive me for a period of one month then **I GIVE, DEVISE AND BEQUEATH** all the rest, residue and remainder of my estate of whatsoever kind and wheresoever situate to my said [spouse]/[partner] absolutely.

SEVENTH: If my said [spouse]/[partner] shall predecease me or shall not survive me for the period aforesaid **I DIRECT** that the previous clause shall not take effect and this my will shall be construed and take effect as if the previous clause had been wholly omitted therefrom and that the remaining clauses of this will shall take effect.

EIGHTH: In so far as it may be necessary and for the avoidance of doubt I direct that if my [spouse]/[partner] shall survive me for a period of less than one month then the income of my estate accruing from the date of my death until the date of the death of my [spouse]/[partner] shall be accumulated and form part of my residuary estate.

NINTH: I give, devise, and bequeath all the rest, residue and remainder of my estate to _____ _____ of _____ and _____ of _____in equal shares. However, in the event that either of the above persons predeceases me or refuses this gift, then I give, devise and bequeath their share of my estate to _____ of _____.

TENTH: In addition to all powers allowable to executors under the laws of this state, my executor shall have the following powers:

(i) to dispose of any property or any interest therein at such times and upon such terms and conditions as shall seem proper and to give good and sufficient instruments of transfer and to receive the proceeds of any such disposition;

(j) to purchase, manage, maintain and insure any property and to lease the same for such periods and on such terms as shall seem advantageous, and if advisable to pay for the value of any improvements made by a tenant under any such lease; to incur, extend or renew mortgage indebtedness; to make ordinary and extraordinary repairs and alterations to any building, to raze or erect buildings and to make improvements or to abandon any buildings or property; and to make any agreement of partition of such property and to give or receive money or other property in connection therewith;

(k) to exercise or sell all rights, options, powers and privileges, and to vote in person or by proxy, in relation to any stocks, bonds or other securities, all as fully as might be done by persons owning similar property in their own right;

(l)   to manage, sell, administer, liquidate, continue or otherwise deal with any corporation, partnership or other business interest received by my trust estate as my Executor deems fit;

(m) to institute, defend, settle or compromise, by arbitration or otherwise, all claims;

(n)   to employ or retain such agents and advisors, including any firm with which any fiduciary may be affiliated, as may seem advisable and to delegate authority thereto, and to compensate them from the funds of my estate provided such compensation is reasonable in the circumstances;

(o)   to settle any entitlement of any beneficiary, in part or in whole, by payment in cash or by the transfer of a specific asset or assets to the beneficiary or to the legal guardian of the beneficiary with power to require the beneficiary or any such guardian to accept such asset or assets at such value or estimate of value as my executor shall (acting reasonably) unilaterally deem fair; and

(p)   to pay all necessary or proper expenses and charges from income or principal, or partly from each, in such manner as may seem equitable.

ELEVENTH: To the extent that provision has not been made under the will for the management of any property, asset or item to be given outright to a person who is a minor, my executor may, without court approval, pay or transfer all or part of such property to a parent or guardian of that minor or that minor's estate, to a custodian under the Uniform Transfers to Minors Act, or may defer payment or transfer of such property until the minor reaches the age of majority, as defined by his or her state of residence. No bond shall be required for such payments.

TWELVETH: I declare that any executor and/or trustee for the time being a lawyer or other person engaged in any profession or business shall be entitled to charge and be paid all usual professional or other reasonable and proper charges for business done or services rendered or time spent by him or his firm in proving this will and administering my estate and in relation to the trusts of the will or of any codicil to it whether in the ordinary course of his profession or business or not and although not of a nature requiring the employment of a lawyer or other professional or business person.

THIRTEENTH: I declare that income received after my death shall be treated as income of my estate regardless of the period to which it relates.

FOURTEENTH: I declare that no executor of this will shall be liable for any loss not attributable to the executor's own dishonesty or to the wilful commission by the executor of any act known to be a breach of executor's duties and obligations as executor.

FIFTEENTH: If any person, whether or not related to me by blood or in any way, shall attempt, either directly or indirectly, to set aside the probate of my will or oppose or contest any of the provisions hereof, then any share or interest in my estate given to that person under my will shall be revoked and, in its stead, I give and bequeath the sum of one dollar ($1.00), only that, and no further interest whatever in my estate to such person.

IN WITNESS HEREOF, I sign the foregoing as my Last Will and Testament, do it willingly and as my free and voluntary act for the purpose herein expressed, this _____ day of _____ 20____.

_____
(Signed)

Signed by the above-named as and for his Last Will and Testament in our presence, each of us being present at the same time who at his request and in his presence and in the presence of each other have hereunto subscribed our names as witnesses.

We, the witnesses, sign our name to this document, and we declare under penalty of perjury, that the foregoing is true and correct, this _____ day of _____, 20____.

Name: _____
Signature: _____
Address: _____
_____
_____
_____

Name: _____
Signature: _____
Address: _____
_____
_____

NINTH WILL

(Married or in a registered domestic partnership with no children (for wife/female partner))

Downloadable Forms

Blank copies of this form can be downloaded from the EstateBee website. Simply login to your account or, if you don't have an account, you can create one for free.

www.estate-bee.com/login

Once logged in, go to your profile page and enter the code listed below in the 'Use Codes' tab:

NinthWill1492B

LAST WILL AND TESTAMENT

OF

_____

I, _____, of _____ in the State of
_____, County of _____, being of sound and disposing
mind and memory and having attained the age of majority in my state, hereby **REVOKE** all former
wills, codicils and other testamentary dispositions at any time heretofore made by me and declare
this to be my last will.

FIRST: [I am married to _____.]/[I am in a registered domestic partnership _____
_____.] I do not have any living children.

SECOND: I appoint _____ of _____ to be executor of this my
will. If this person or institution shall for any reason be unable or unwilling to act (at any time)
as my executor, then I appoint _____ of _____ to be my
executor of my will. No executor appointed hereunder shall be required to post bond.

THIRD: I direct my executor to pay all my just debts (which are capable of enforcement against
me), funeral and testamentary expenses as soon as practical after my death.

FOURTH: I give, devise, and bequeath _____ to
_____ of _____ absolutely.

FIFTH: I give, devise, and bequeath _____ to
_____ of _____ absolutely.

*[Repeat or delete as necessary to make further specific gifts/bequests. Note you may need to renumber
subsequent clauses]*

SIXTH: If my [spouse]/[partner], _____, shall survive me for a
period of one month then **I GIVE, DEVISE AND BEQUEATH** all the rest, residue and remainder of
my estate of whatsoever kind and wheresoever situate to my said [spouse]/[partner] absolutely.

SEVENTH: If my said [spouse]/[partner] shall predecease me or shall not survive me for the period aforesaid **I DIRECT** that the previous clause shall not take effect and this my will shall be construed and take effect as if the previous clause had been wholly omitted therefrom and that the remaining clauses of this will shall take effect.

EIGHTH: In so far as it may be necessary and for the avoidance of doubt I direct that if my [spouse]/[partner] shall survive me for a period of less than one month then the income of my estate accruing from the date of my death until the date of the death of my [spouse]/[partner] shall be accumulated and form part of my residuary estate.

NINTH: I give, devise, and bequeath all the rest, residue and remainder of my estate to
_____ of _____
and _____ of _____in equal shares.
However, in the event that either of the above persons predeceases me or refuses this gift, then I give, devise and bequeath their share of my estate to
_____ of _____.

TENTH: In addition to all powers allowable to executors under the laws of this state, my executor shall have the following powers:

(i)   to dispose of any property or any interest therein at such times and upon such terms and conditions as shall seem proper and to give good and sufficient instruments of transfer and to receive the proceeds of any such disposition;

(j)   to purchase, manage, maintain and insure any property and to lease the same for such periods and on such terms as shall seem advantageous, and if advisable to pay for the value of any improvements made by a tenant under any such lease; to incur, extend or renew mortgage indebtedness; to make ordinary and extraordinary repairs and alterations to any building, to raze or erect buildings and to make improvements or to abandon any buildings or property; and to make any agreement of partition of such property and to give or receive money or other property in connection therewith;

(k)   to exercise or sell all rights, options, powers and privileges, and to vote in person or by proxy, in relation to any stocks, bonds or other securities, all as fully as might be done by persons owning similar property in their own right;

(l)   to manage, sell, administer, liquidate, continue or otherwise deal with any corporation, partnership or other business interest received by my trust estate as my Executor deems fit;

(m) to institute, defend, settle or compromise, by arbitration or otherwise, all claims;

(n) to employ or retain such agents and advisors, including any firm with which any fiduciary may be affiliated, as may seem advisable and to delegate authority thereto, and to compensate them from the funds of my estate provided such compensation is reasonable in the circumstances;

(o) to settle any entitlement of any beneficiary, in part or in whole, by payment in cash or by the transfer of a specific asset or assets to the beneficiary or to the legal guardian of the beneficiary with power to require the beneficiary or any such guardian to accept such asset or assets at such value or estimate of value as my executor shall (acting reasonably) unilaterally deem fair; and

(p) to pay all necessary or proper expenses and charges from income or principal, or partly from each, in such manner as may seem equitable.

ELEVENTH: To the extent that provision has not been made under the will for the management of any property, asset or item to be given outright to a person who is a minor, my executor may, without court approval, pay or transfer all or part of such property to a parent or guardian of that minor or that minor's estate, to a custodian under the Uniform Transfers to Minors Act, or may defer payment or transfer of such property until the minor reaches the age of majority, as defined by his or her state of residence. No bond shall be required for such payments.

TWELVETH: I declare that any executor and/or trustee for the time being a lawyer or other person engaged in any profession or business shall be entitled to charge and be paid all usual professional or other reasonable and proper charges for business done or services rendered or time spent by him or his firm in proving this will and administering my estate and in relation to the trusts of the will or of any codicil to it whether in the ordinary course of his profession or business or not and although not of a nature requiring the employment of a lawyer or other professional or business person.

THIRTEENTH: I declare that income received after my death shall be treated as income of my estate regardless of the period to which it relates.

FOURTEENTH: I declare that no executor of this will shall be liable for any loss not attributable to the executor's own dishonesty or to the wilful commission by the executor of any act known to be a breach of executor's duties and obligations as executor.

FIFTEENTH: If any person, whether or not related to me by blood or in any way, shall attempt, either directly or indirectly, to set aside the probate of my will or oppose or contest any of the provisions hereof, then any share or interest in my estate given to that person under my will shall be revoked and, in its stead, I give and bequeath the sum of one dollar ($1.00), only that, and no further interest whatever in my estate to such person.

IN WITNESS HEREOF, I sign the foregoing as my Last Will and Testament, do it willingly and as my free and voluntary act for the purpose herein expressed, this _____ day of _____ 20_____.

_____

(Signed)

Signed by the above-named as and for her Last Will and Testament in our presence, each of us being present at the same time who at her request and in her presence and in the presence of each other have hereunto subscribed our names as witnesses.

We, the witnesses, sign our name to this document, and we declare under penalty of perjury, that the foregoing is true and correct, this _____ day of _____, 20_____.

Name: _____
Signature: _____
Address: _____
_____
_____

Name: _____
Signature: _____
Address: _____
_____
_____

Appendix 4

General Instructions for Completing Your Will

Appendix 4

General Instructions for Completing your Will

1. Carefully read all the instructions below and select the will from Appendix 3 which is most suitable to your circumstances.

2. Carefully consider who will act as your executors, trustees, witnesses, and guardians (if any). Carefully consider who will be the proposed beneficiaries. When inputting the details in your will, you must be as specific as possible and avoid broad statements such as "my friends".

3. Print out the will form which you intend using and complete it neatly using a pen or carefully edit the text version of the form (that is available to you to download) on your computer.

4. The will should be completed in accordance with the special instructions in Appendix 5 below.

5. Do not leave any blank spaces.

6. Arrange for your witnesses and you to meet with a Notary. Remember, in Vermont, you will need three witnesses instead of two.

7. Do not sign the will or the Affidavit until you and the witnesses are with the Notary.

8. Sign both the will and the Affidavit in the Notary's presence and have your witnesses do likewise.

9. Have the Notary notarize the will and Affidavit.

NOTE In the event that you do not want to execute a self-proving affidavit, for whatever reason, you and your witnesses are free to execute the will otherwise than in the presence of a Notary. Again, only in the state of Louisiana must you have a will notarized. You must sign your will in the presence of all witnesses.

Appendix 5

Specific Instructions for Completing Your Will

Appendix 5

Specific Instructions for Completing your Will

Instructions for completion of First Will document

1. Fill in your name in the space provided in the title "last will and testament of ____".

2. Fill in your name and address in the space provided in the first paragraph.

3. In the paragraph entitled "Second", fill in the name and address of your executor and the name and address of your alternate executor. **

4. In the paragraphs entitled "Fourth" and "Fifth", fill in the names and addresses of the proposed beneficiary of each specific gift and details of that specific gift. Add or delete gift clauses as you require but remember to re-number the subsequent clause numbers as appropriate.

5. In the paragraph entitled "Sixth", fill in the name and address of the sole beneficiary of your estate and the name and address of your alternate beneficiary.

6. Now Go to Number 4 in the General Instructions.

Instructions for completion of Second Will document

1. Fill in your name in the space provided in the title "last will and testament of ____".

2. Fill in your name and address in the space provided in the first paragraph.

3. In the paragraph entitled "Second", fill in the name and address of your executor and the name and address of your alternate executor. **

4. In the paragraphs entitled "Fourth" and "Fifth", fill in the names and addresses of the proposed beneficiary of each specific gift and details of that specific gift. Add or delete gift clauses as you require but remember to re-number the subsequent clause numbers as appropriate.

5. In the paragraph entitled "Sixth", fill in the name and address of the two beneficiaries of your estate and the name and address of your alternate beneficiary. You can add more beneficiaries if you wish but remember to state the share of the residuary estate which they will be entitled to.

6. Now Go to Number 4 in the General Instructions.

Instructions for completion of Third Will document

1. Fill in your name in the space provided in the title "last will and testament of ____".

2. Fill in your name and address in the space provided in the first paragraph.

3. In the paragraph entitled "First", specify the number of children you have and the names of each child.

4. In the paragraph entitled "Second", fill in the name and address of your executor and the name and address of your alternate executor. **

5. In the paragraph entitled "Fourth", fill in the name and address of the each of the two proposed guardians of your minor children.

6. In the paragraphs entitled "Fifth" and "Sixth", fill in the names and addresses of the proposed beneficiary of each specific gift and details of that specific gift. Add or delete gift clauses as you require but remember to re-number the subsequent clause numbers as appropriate.

7. In the paragraph entitled "Seventh", fill in the age at which your children should receive their inheritance, for example, eighteen or twenty-one. This will need to be inserted in two places in this clause.

8. Now Go to Number 4 in the General Instructions.

Instructions for completion of Fourth & Fifth Will documents

1. Fill in your name in the space provided in the title "last will and testament of ____".

2. Fill in your name and address in the space provided in the first paragraph.

3. In the paragraph entitled "First", enter the name of your spouse or partner (and delete the section in square brackets regarding the spouse or partner which is not relevant to your situation) and then specify the number of children you have and the names of each child. Remember to remove all square brackets.

4. In the paragraph entitled "Second", fill in the name and address of your executor and the name and address of your alternate executor. **

5. In the paragraphs entitled "Fourth" and "Fifth", fill in the names and addresses of the proposed beneficiary of each specific gift and details of that specific gift. Add or delete gift clauses as you require but remember to re-number the subsequent clause numbers as appropriate.

6. In the paragraph entitled "Sixth", fill in the name of your spouse or partner and delete the part of the text "[spouse]/[partner]" which is not relevant to your situation – so that the text only reads either spouse or partner, as the case may be. You will need to make this deletion in two places in this clause. Remember to remove all square brackets.

7. In the paragraph entitled "Seventh", delete the part of the text "[spouse]/[partner]" which is not relevant to your situation – so that the text only reads either spouse or partner, as the case may be. You will need to make this deletion in one place only in this clause. Remember to remove all square brackets.

8. In the paragraph entitled "Eighth", delete the part of the text "[spouse]/[partner]" which is not relevant to your situation – so that the text only reads either spouse or partner, as the case may be. You will need to make this deletion in two places in this clause. Remember to remove all square brackets.

9. In the paragraph entitled "Ninth", fill in the name and address of each of the beneficiaries of your estate who will benefit should your spouse or partner predecease you or fail to survive you by a period of one month.

10. Now Go to Number 4 in the General Instructions.

Instructions for completion of Sixth and Seventh Will documents

1. Fill in your name in the space provided in the title "last will and testament of ____".

2. Fill in your name and address in the space provided in the first paragraph.

3. In the paragraph entitled "First", enter the name of your spouse or partner (and delete the section in square brackets regarding the spouse or partner which is not relevant to your situation) and then specify the number of children you have and the names of each child. Remember to remove all square brackets.

4. In the paragraph entitled "Second", fill in the name and address of your executor and the name and address of your alternate executor. **

5. In the paragraph entitled "Fourth", fill in the names and addresses of the proposed guardians of your infant children.

6. In the paragraphs entitled "Fifth" and "Sixth", fill in the names and addresses of the proposed beneficiary of each specific gift and details of that specific gift. Add or delete gift clauses as you require but remember to re-number the subsequent clause numbers as appropriate.

7. In the paragraph entitled "Seventh", fill in the name of your spouse or partner and delete the part of the text "[spouse]/[partner]" which is not relevant to your situation – so that the text only reads either spouse or partner, as the case may be. You will need to make this deletion in two places in this clause. Remember to remove all square brackets.

8. In the paragraph entitled "Eighth", delete the part of the text "[spouse]/[partner]" which is not relevant to your situation – so that the text only reads either spouse or partner, as the case

may be. You will need to make this deletion in one place only in this clause. Remember to remove all square brackets.

9. In the paragraph entitled "Ninth", delete the part of the text "[spouse]/[partner]" which is not relevant to your situation – so that the text only reads either spouse or partner, as the case may be. You will need to make this deletion in two places in this clause. Remember to remove all square brackets.

10. In the paragraph entitled "Tenth", fill in the age at which your children should receive their inheritance, for example, eighteen or twenty-one. This will need to be entered in two places in this clause.

11. Now Go to Number 4 in the General Instructions.

Instructions for completion of Eight & Ninth Will documents

1. Fill in your name in the space provided in the title "last will and testament of ____".

2. Fill in your name and address in the space provided in the first paragraph.

3. In the paragraph entitled "First", enter the name of your spouse or partner (and delete the section in square brackets regarding the spouse or partner which is not relevant to your situation). Remember to remove all square brackets.

4. In the paragraph entitled "Second", fill in the name and address of your executor and the name and address of your alternate executor. **

5. In the paragraphs entitled "Fourth" and "Fifth", fill in the names and addresses of the proposed beneficiary of each specific gift and details of that specific gift. Add or delete gift clauses as you require but remember to re-number the subsequent clause numbers as appropriate.

6. In the paragraph entitled "Sixth", fill in the name of your spouse or partner and delete the part of the text "[spouse]/[partner]" which is not relevant to your situation – so that the text only reads either spouse or partner, as the case may be. You will need to make this deletion in two

places in this clause. Remember to remove all square brackets.

7. In the paragraph entitled "Seventh", delete the part of the text "[spouse]/[partner]" which is not relevant to your situation – so that the text only reads either spouse or partner, as the case may be. You will need to make this deletion in one place only in this clause. Remember to remove all square brackets.

8. In the paragraph entitled "Eighth", delete the part of the text "[spouse]/[partner]" which is not relevant to your situation – so that the text only reads either spouse or partner, as the case may be. You will need to make this deletion in two places in this clause. Remember to remove all square brackets.

9. In the paragraph entitled "Ninth", fill in the name and address of each of the beneficiaries of your estate who will benefit should your spouse or partner predecease you or fail to survive you by a period of one month.

10. Now Go to Number 4 in the General Instructions.

Note: Three Witnesses are required for wills executed in Vermont. In every other state, only two witnesses are required. Notarization is not required in any state other than Louisiana. You may need to amend your documents accordingly.

** Executors: Note, you may wish to appoint two executors (and two substitute executors) to act jointly. In this case, simply add the name and address of the second executor such that the sentence specifies that you appoint Person 1 and Person 2 to act as executors.

Appendix 6

Self-Proving Affidavit – Type 1

Downloadable Forms

Blank copies of this form can be downloaded from the EstateBee website. Simply login to your account or, if you don't have an account, you can create one for free.

www.estate-bee.com/login

Once logged in, go to your profile page and enter the code listed below in the 'Use Codes' tab:

Affidavit11492B

Appendix 6

Self-Proving Affidavit – Type 1

For Use in The Following States:

Alabama	Indiana	North Dakota
Alaska	Maine	Oregon
Arizona	Mississippi	South Carolina
Arkansas	Montana	South Dakota
Colorado	Nebraska	Tennessee
Hawaii	Nevada	Utah
Idaho	New Mexico	Washington
Illinois	New York	West Virginia

Self-Proving Affidavit

State of _____   County of _____

We,_____, _____,

and _____,

the testator and the witnesses respectively, whose names are signed to the attached instrument in those capacities, personally appearing before the undersigned authority and first being duly sworn, do hereby declare to the undersigned authority under penalty of perjury that the testator declared, signed, and executed the instrument as his/her last will; he/she signed it willingly or willingly directed another to sign for him/her; he/she executed it as his/her free and voluntary act for the purposes therein expressed; and each of the witnesses, at the request of the testator, in his or her hearing and presence, and in the presence of each other, signed the will as witness and that to the best of his or her knowledge the testator was at that time eighteen (18) years of age or older, of sound mind and under no constraint or undue influence.

_____ [Signature of Testator]

_____ [Printed or typed name of Testator]

_____ [Address of Testator, Line 1]

_____ [Address of Testator, Line 2]

_____ [Signature of Witness #1]

_____ [Printed or typed name of Witness #1]

_____ [Address of Witness #1, Line 1]

_____ [Address of Witness #1, Line 2]

_____ [Signature of Witness #2]

_____ [Printed or typed name of Witness #2]

_____ [Address of Witness #2, Line 1]

_____ [Address of Witness #2, Line 2]

Subscribed, sworn, and acknowledged before me, _____, a notary
public, by _____, the testator, and
by _____, and
_____, the witnesses, this _____
_____ day of _____, 20 ____.

[Notarial Seal]

_____

Notary Public's Signature

My Commission Expires: _____

Appendix 7

Self-Proving Affidavit – Type 2

Downloadable Forms

Blank copies of this form can be downloaded from the EstateBee website. Simply login to your account or, if you don't have an account, you can create one for free.

www.estate-bee.com/login

Once logged in, go to your profile page and enter the code listed below in the 'Use Codes' tab:

Affidavit21492B

Appendix 7

Self-Proving Affidavit – Type 2

For Use in The Following States:

Delaware	Kentucky	Oklahoma
Florida	Massachusetts	Pennsylvania
Georgia	Missouri	Rhode Island
Iowa	New Jersey	Virginia
Kansas	North Carolina	Wyoming

Self-Proving Affidavit

State of _____   County of _____

I, the undersigned, an officer authorized to administer oaths, certify that
_____, the testator, and _____
, and _____, the witnesses, whose names are signed to the attached
or foregoing instrument and whose signatures appear below, having appeared together before
me and having been first duly sworn, each then declare to me that the attached or foregoing
instrument is the last will of the testator; the testator willingly and voluntarily declared, signed
and executed the will or willingly directed another to sign in the presence of the witnesses; the
witnesses signed the will upon request by the testator, in the presence and hearing of the testator,
and in the presence of each other; to the best knowledge of each witness the testator was, at the
time of the signing, eighteen (18) years of age or older, of sound mind, and under no constraint or
undue influence; and each witness was and is competent, and of the proper age to witness a will.

_____ [Signature of Testator]
_____ [Printed or typed name of Testator]
_____ [Address of Testator, Line 1]
_____ [Address of Testator, Line 2]

_____ [Signature of Witness #1]

_____ [Printed or typed name of Witness #1]

_____ [Address of Witness #1, Line 1]

_____ [Address of Witness #1, Line 2]

_____ [Signature of Witness #2]

_____ [Printed or typed name of Witness #2]

_____ [Address of Witness #2, Line 1]

_____ [Address of Witness #2, Line 2]

Subscribed, sworn, and acknowledged before me, _____,

a notary public, by _____

, the testator, and by _____, and

_____, the witnesses, this _____ day of

_____, 20 ___.

Signed:

_____

_____

Official Capacity of Officer

Appendix 8

Self-Proving Affidavit – Type 3 - Texas

Downloadable Forms

Blank copies of this form can be downloaded from the EstateBee website. Simply login to your account or, if you don't have an account, you can create one for free.

www.estate-bee.com/login

Once logged in, go to your profile page and enter the code listed below in the 'Use Codes' tab:

Affidavit31492B

Self-Proving Affidavit

State of Texas   County of _____

Before me, the undersigned authority, on this day personally appeared

_____, _____, and

_____, known to me to be the testator and the witnesses,

respectively, whose names are subscribed to the annexed or foregoing instrument in their respective capacities, and, all of said persons being by me duly sworn, the said

_____, testator, declared to me and to the said witnesses in my presence that said instrument is his last will and testament, and that he had willingly made and executed it as his free act and deed; and the said witnesses, each on his oath stated to me, in the presence and hearing of the said testator, that the said testator had declared to them that said instrument is his last will and testament, and that he executed same as such and wanted each of them to sign it as a witness; and upon their oaths each witness stated further that they did sign the same as witnesses in the presence of the said testator and at his request; that he was at that time eighteen years of age or over (or being under such age, was or had been lawfully married, or was then a member of the armed forces of the United States or of an auxiliary thereof or of the Maritime Service) and was of sound mind; and that each of said witnesses was then at least fourteen years of age.

_____
Testator

_____
Witness

_____
Witness

Subscribed and sworn to before me by the said _____, testator,

and by the said _____ and

_____, witnesses, this _____ day of _____

_____, 20 ___.

(SEAL)

(Signed)

_____,

_____
(Official Capacity of Officer

Appendix 9

Additional Clauses That You May Wish to Add

Downloadable Forms

Blank copies of this form can be downloaded from the EstateBee website. Simply login to your account or, if you don't have an account, you can create one for free.

www.estate-bee.com/login

Once logged in, go to your profile page and enter the code listed below in the 'Use Codes' tab:

WillClauses1492B

Appendix 9

Additional Clauses That You May Wish to Add

Appointing a custodian under UTMA

All property left under this Will to _____[insert name of child], the management of which is not hereby otherwise provided for shall be given to _____[insert name of primary custodian] of _____[insert address of primary custodian], in the capacity of custodian under the _____[insert state in which you are resident] Uniform Transfers to Minors Act, to hold until _____[insert name of child] reaches _____[insert age based on UTMA requirements] years of age. If _____[insert name of custodian], is unwilling or unable to serve as custodian for any reason, then I appoint _____[insert name of alternate custodian] of _____[insert address of alternate custodian] to serve as custodian instead.

Appointing an alternate beneficiary for a specific gift

I give, devise, and bequeath _____ to _____ of _____ absolutely. If this person is unable or unwilling to accept this gift (for any reason) then I give same to _____ of _____ absolutely.

Releasing someone from a debt

I release and forgive _____ of _____ and should he/she predecease me his/her personal representatives and estate from all debt due to me at the date of my death and from all interest due in respect thereof.

Or

I release and forgive _____ of _____ and should he/she predecease me his/her personal representatives and estate from the debt of $ _____ and from all interest due in respect thereof.

Nominating assets to be sold to pay taxes

I direct my executors to pay all estate, inheritance and succession taxes (including any interest and penalties thereon) payable by reason of my death using the following asset(s):- _____ _____.

Nominating assets to be sold to pay debts

I direct my executors to pay my enforceable unsecured debts and funeral expenses, the expenses of my last illness, and the expenses of administering my estate using the following asset(s):- _____ _____.

Burial clause

I direct that my executors should bury me at [insert name and address of cemetery].

Cremation clause

I desire that my body be cremated in the crematorium at [insert name and address of crematorium]. I further direct that my ashes be [insert details of what should be done with your ashes].

EstateBee's Estate Planning Range

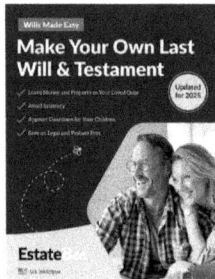

Make Your Own Last Will & Testament

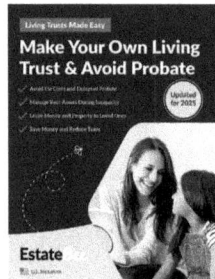

Make Your Own Living Trust & Avoid Probate

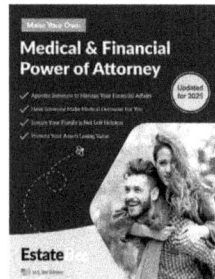

Make Your Own Medical & Financial Power of Attorney

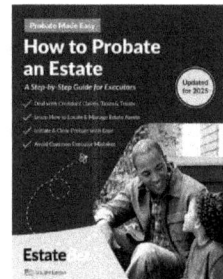

How to Probate an Estate - A Step-by-Step Guide for Executors

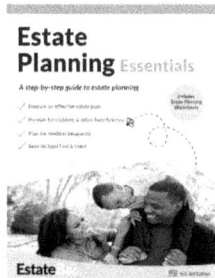

Estate Planning Essentials - A Step-by-Step Guide to Estate Planning

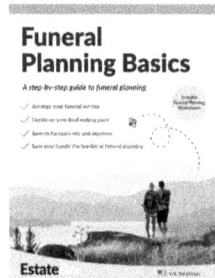

Funeral Planning Basics – A Step-by-Step Guide to Funeral Planning

Legal Will Kit

Living Trust Kit

Healthcare Power of Attorney & Living Will Kit

Codicil to a Last Will & Testament Kit

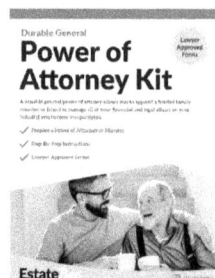

Durable General Power of Attorney Kit

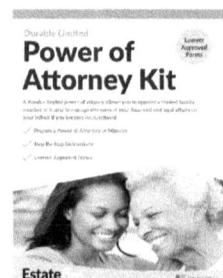

Durable Limited Power of Attorney Kit

EstateBee's Online Will Writer

Create Your Estate Planning Documents Online in Minutes...

EstateBee's online software enables you to create bespoke estate planning documents such as wills, living trusts, living wills and powers of attorney from the comfort of your own home.

The software uses documents which have been pre-approved by experienced estate planning lawyers and are tailored to comply with the individual laws of each state (except Louisiana).

Using a simple question and answer process, you'll be able to create a document which is bespoke to your individual circumstances. The process only takes a few minutes and help, and information are available at every step.

Get Started Online Now

Why choose EstateBee's Online Will Writer

✓ Save Time and Money

✓ Created by Experienced Attorneys

✓ Advanced Features

✓ Compliant with US Laws

✓ Bank Level Encryption

✓ 20+ years in Business

Proud to have helped thousands of people make wills, trusts, and powers of attorney online over the past 20 years.

Estate

About EstateBee

EstateBee, the internationally recognized publisher of estate planning products, was founded in 2000 by lawyers from one of the most prestigious international law firms in the world. Its aim was simple – to provide access to quality legal information and products at an affordable price.

www.ingramcontent.com/pod-product-compliance
Lightning Source LLC
Chambersburg PA
CBHW062025210326
41519CB00060B/7078